Sir David Lyndesay's Works

Part IV

Elibron Classics
www.elibron.com

Early English Text Society.

Sir David Lyndesay's Works, Part IV.

Ane Satyre
of the thrie Estaits,

IN COMMENDATION OF VERTEW

AND VITVPERATION OF VYCE.

MAID BE

Sir Dauid Lindesay of the Mont,

ALIAS,

Lyon King of Armes.

AT EDINBVRGH.

PRINTED BE ROBERT CHARTERIS.

1602.

CVM PRIVILEGIO REGIS.

EDITED BY F. HALL, ESQ., D.C.L.

LONDON:

PUBLISHED FOR THE EARLY ENGLISH TEXT SOCIETY,

BY N. TRÜBNER & CO., 60, PATERNOSTER ROW.

MDCCCLXIX.

Price Four Shillings.

3

Early English Text Society.

The Publications for the first three years, 1864, 1865, and 1866, are out of print, but a separate subscription has been opened for their immediate reprint, and the Texts for 1864 are now at press. Subscribers who desire all or any of these years should send their names at once to the Hon. Secretary, as one hundred additional names are required before the Texts for 1865 can be sent to press.

The Publications for 1864 are:—
1. Early English Alliterative Poems, ab. 1360 A.D., ed. R. Morris.
2. Arthur, ab. 1440, ed. F. J. Furnivall.
3. Lauder on the Dewtie of Kyngis, &c., 1556, ed. F. Hall.
4. Sir Gawayne and the Green Knight, ab. 1360, ed. R. Morris.

The Publications for 1865 are:—
5. Hume's Orthographie and Congruitie of the Britan Tongue, ab. 1617, ed. H. B. Wheatley.
6. Lancelot of the Laik, ab. 1500, ed. Rev. W. W. Skeat.
7. Genesis and Exodus, ab. 1250, ed. R. Morris.
8. Morte Arthure, ab. 1440, Rev. G. G. Perry.
9. Thynne on Chaucer's Works, ab. 1598, ed. Dr Kingsley.
10. Merlin, ab. 1450, Part I., ed. H. B. Wheatley.
11. Lyndesay's Monarche, &c., 1552, Part I., ed. F. Hall.
12. Wright's Chaste Wife, ab. 1462, ed. F. J. Furnivall.

The Publications for 1866 are:—
13. Seinte Marherete, 1200-1330, ed. Rev. O. Cockayne.
14. Kyng Horn, Floris and Blancheflour, &c., ed. Rev. J. R. Lumby.
15. Political, Religious, and Love Poems, ed. F. J. Furnivall.
16. The Book of Quinte Essence, ab. 1460-70, ed. F. J. Furnivall.
17. Parallel Extracts from 29 MSS. of Piers Plowman, ed. Rev. W. W. Skeat.
18. Hali Meidenhad, ab. 1200, ed. Rev. O. Cockayne.
19. Lyndesay's Monarche, &c., Part II., ed. F. Hall.
20. Hampole's English Prose Treatises, ed. Rev. G. G. Perry.
21. Merlin, Part II., ed. H. B. Wheatley.
22. Partenay or Lusignen, ed. Rev. W. W. Skeat.
23. Dan Michel's Ayenbite of Inwyt, 1340, ed. R. Morris.

The Publications for 1867 are:—
24. Hymns to the Virgin and Christ; the Parliament of Devils, &c., ab. 1430. ed. F. J. Furnivall. 3s.
25. The Stacions of Rome, the Pilgrims' Sea-voyage, with Clene Maydenhod, ed. F. J. Furnivall. 1s.
26. Religious Pieces in Prose and Verse, from R. Thornton's MS. (ab. 1440), ed. Rev. G. G. Perry. 2s.
27. Levins's Manipulus Vocabulorum, 1570, ed. H. B. Wheatley. 12s.
28. Langland's Vision of Piers Plowman, 1362 A.D. Part I. The earliest or Vernon Text; Text A. ed. Rev. W. W. Skeat. 6s.
29. Early English Homilies (ab. 1220-30 A.D.) from unique MSS. in the Lambeth and other Libraries. Part I. Edited by R. Morris. 7s.
30. Pierce the Ploughmans Crede, ed. Rev. W. W. Skeat. 1s.

The Publications for 1868 (one guinea) are:—
31. Myrc's Duties of a Parish Priest, in Verse, ab. 1420 A.D., ed. E. Peacock. 4s.
32. The Babees Book, Urbanitatis, the Bokes of Norture of John Russell and Hugh Rhodes, the Bokes of Keruyng, Curtasye, and Demeanour, &c., with some French and Latin Poems on like subjects, ed. from Harleian and other MSS. by F. J. Furnivall. 15s.
33. The Knight de la Tour Landry (from French of A.D. 1372), ab. 1440 A.D. A Father's Book for his Daughters, ed. from Harl. MS. 1764 and Caxton's version, by Thomas Wright. 8s.
34. Early English Homilies (before 1300 A.D.) from unique MSS. in the Lambeth and other Libraries. Part II., ed. R. Morris, Esq. 8s.
35. Lyndesay's Works, Part III.: The Historie and Testament of Squyer Meldrum, ed. F. Hall. 2s.

A few copies are left of No. 5, Hume's Orthographie, 4s.; No. 17, Extracts from Piers Plowman, 1s.; No. 20, Hampole's Treatises, 2s.; No. 22, Partenay, 6s.; 23, Ayenbite, 10s. 6d.

The Society's Report, January, 1869, with Lists of Texts to be published in future years, etc., etc., can be had on application to the Hon. Secretary, HENRY B. WHEATLEY, Esq., 53, Berners Street, W.

4

Ane Satyre

of the thrie Estaits,

IN COMMENDATION OF VERTEW

AND VITVPERATION OF VYCE.

MAID BE

Sir Dauid Lindesay of the Mont,

ALIAS,

Lyon King of Armes.

AT EDINBVRGH.

PRINTED BE ,ROBERT CHARTERIS.

1602.

CVM PRIVILEGIO REGIS.

PLEASANT SATYRE

OF THE THRIE ESTAITIS,

IN COMMENDATIOVN OF VERTEW AND VITVPERATIOVN OF VYCE:

AS FOLLOWIS.

DILIGENCE.

THE Father and founder of faith and felicitie, — *May God the Father,*
That ȝour fassioun formed to his similitude,
And his Sone, our Sauiour, scheild in necessitie,— *God the Son,*
4 That bocht ȝow from baillis ranson rude, *Who ransomed us*
Repleadgeand his presonaris with his hart- *with his*
    blude,— *blood,*
The halie Gaist, gouernour and grounder of grace, *and God the Holy Ghost,*
Of wisdome and weilfair baith fontaine and flude,
8 Gif ȝow all that I sie seasit in this place, *protect and*
    And scheild ȝow from sinne, *inspire you with*
And with his Spreit ȝow inspyre, *His Spirit, till*
Till I haue shawin my desyre.
12 Silence, Soueraine, I requyre; *you have heard*
    For now I begin. *my poem!*

Tak tent to me, my freinds, and hald ȝow coy; *My friends,*
    For I am sent to ȝow, as messingeir, *I present myself*
16 From ane nobill and rycht redoubtit Roy,
The quhilk hes bene absent this monie ȝeir,— *as messenger from*
Humanitie, giue ȝe his name wald speir,— *King Humanity,*
Quha bade me shaw to ȝow, but variance, *who will soon appear among you,*
20 That he intendis amang ȝow to compeir,

7

in triumph

With ane triumph and awfull ordinance,
With crown, and sword, and scepter in his hand,

and in array,

Temperit with mercie, quhen penitence appeiris ;

24 Howbeit that hee lang tyme hes bene sleipand,

to avenge misrule

Quhairthrow misreull hes rung thir monie ӡeiris,

and the death of

That innocentis hes bene brocht on thair beiris

innocent folk.

Be fals reporteris of this natioun :

A reform

28 Thocht ӡoung oppressouris at the elder leiris,

is coming.

Be now assurit of reformatioun.

Misdoers,

Sie no misdoeris be sa bauld

depart;

As to remaine into this hauld ;

or you will be

32 For quhy, be him that Iudas sauld,

hanged.

Thay will be heich hangit.

Faithful men may sing.

Now faithfull folk for ioy may sing,
For quhy it is the iust bidding

The King says none shall be wronged.

36 Of my soveraine lord the king,
That na man be wrangit.

But excuse him,

Thocht he ane quhyll, into his flouris,
Be gouernit be vylde trompouris,

if he is vicious

40 And sumtyme lufe his paramouris,

meantime,

Hauld ӡe him excusit ;

and avoids

For, quhen he meittis with Correctioun,

Correction,

With Veritie, and Discretioun,

Truth, and

44 Thay will be banisched aff the toun,

Discretion.

Quhilk hes him abusit.

In the King's name, I summon

And heir, be oppin proclamatioun,
I wairne, in name of his magnificence,

the Three Estates

48 The thrie estaitis of this natioun,

to appear

That thay compeir, with detfull diligence,

and do homage,—

And till his grace mak thair obedience.

the spirituality, the burgesses, and the temporal peers.

And, first, I wairne the Spritualitie ;

52 And sie the burgessis spair not for expence,
Bot speid thame heir, with Temporalitie.

Als, I beseik ӡow famous auditouris,

Hearers,

Conveinit in this congregatioun,

be patient,

56 To be patient the space of certaine houris,

8

Till ȝe haue hard our short narratioun. *and disdain not*
And, als, we mak ȝow supplicatioun, *my words,*
That na man tak our wordis intill disdaine, *though the*
60 Althocht ȝe hear, be declamatioun, *Commonwealth*
The common-weill richt pitiouslie complaine. *complain, though*
Rycht so the verteous ladie Veritie *Truth*
Will mak ane pitious lamentatioun ;
64 Als for the treuth sho will impresonit be, *be imprisoned.*
And banischit lang tyme out of the toun.
And Chastitie will mak narratioun, *and though*
How sho can get na ludging in this land, *Chastity be*
68 Till that the heauinlie king Correctioun *banished.*
Meit with the king and commoun, hand for hand.
    Prudent peopill, I pray ȝow all, *I shall speak*
    Tak na man greif in speciall ; *generally, not of*
72   For wee sall speik in generall, *individuals,*
    For pastyme and for play. *for diversion.*
    Thairfoir, till all our rymis be rung, *So let*
    And our mistoinit sangis be sung, *every man hold*
76   Let euerie man keip weill ane toung, *his one tougue,*
    And euerie woman tway. *and every woman two.*

REX HVMANITAS.

O Lord of Lords, and King of kingis all, *Lord Almighty,*
Omnipotent of power, Prince but peir, *reigning in*
80 Euer ringand in gloir Celestial,— *glory,*
Quha, be great micht, and haifing na mateir, *Maker of all from*
Maid heauin and eird, fyre, air, and watter cleir,— *nothing,*
Send me thy grace, with peace perpetuall, *send me grace*
84 That I may rewll my realme to thy pleaseir ; *to rule as pleases*
Syne, bring my saull to ioy angelicall. *Thee ; and save*
Sen thow hes giuin mee dominatioun *me at last.*
And rewll of pepill subiect to my cure, *If I govern not*
88 Be I nocht rewlit be counsall and ressoun, *aright, my*
In dignitie I may nocht lang indure. *power will be*
I grant, my stait my self may nocht assure, *short-lived.*

Nor ȝit conserue my life in sickernes.

92   Haue pitie, Lord, on mee, thy creature,

Supportand me in all my busines.

I thee requeist, quha rent wes on the Rude,

Me to defend from the deids of defame,

96   That my pepill report of me bot gude,

And be my saifgaird baith from sin and shame.

I knaw my dayis induris bot as ane dreame :

Thairfoir, O Lord, I hairtlie the exhort,

100   To gif me grace to vse my diadeame

To thy pleasure and to my great comfort.

WANTONNES.

My Soueraine Lord and Prince but peir,

Quhat garris ȝow mak sic dreirie cheir ?

104   Be blyth, sa lang as ȝe ar heir,

And pas tyme with pleasure :

For als lang leifis the mirrie man

As the sorie, for ocht he can.

108   His banis full sair, Sir, sall I ban,

That dois ȝow displeasure.

Sa lang as Placebo and I

Remainis into ȝour company,

112   Ȝour grace sall leif richt mirrely :

Of this haif ȝe na dout.

Sa lang as ȝe haue vs in cure,

Ȝour grace, sir, sall want na pleasure.

116   War Solace heir, I ȝow assure,

He wald reioyce this rout.

PLACEBO.

Gude brother myne, quhair is Solace,

The mirrour of all mirrines ?

120   I haue great meruell, be the Mes,

He taries sa lang.

Byde he away, wee ar bot shent :

I ferlie how he fra vs went ;
124 I trow he hes impediment
    That lettis him nocht gang.

Something must
have hindered
his coming.

WANTONNES.

I left Solace, that same greit loun,
Drinkand into the burrows toun :
128 It will cost him halfe of ane croun,
    . Althocht he had na mair.
And, als, he said hee wald gang see
Fair ladie Sensualitie,
132 The buriall of all bewtie
    And portratour preclair.

I left him
drinking;
and he
said he was
going to see Lady
Sensuality, the
dainty beauty.

PLACEBO.

Be God, I see him, at the last,
As he war chaist, rynnand richt fast ;
136 He glowris, euin as he war agast,
    Or fleyit of ane gaist.
Na, he is wod drunkin, I trow.
Se ȝe not that he is wod fow ?
140 I ken weill, be his creischie mow,
    He hes bene at ane feast.

When last I saw
him, he was
running hard, as
if scared by a
ghost.

But no ; he is

mad-drunk,

after a feast.

SOLACE.

Now, quha saw euer sic ane thrang ?
Me thocht sum said I had gaine wrang.
144 Had I help, I wald sing ane sang
    With ane rycht mirrie noyse.
I haue sic pleasour at my hart,
That garris me sing the troubill pairt,
148 Wald sum gude fellow fill the quart,
    It wald my hairt reioyce.
Howbeit my coat be short and nippit,
Thankis be to God, I am weill hippit,
152 Thocht all my gold may shone be grippit
    Intill ane pennie pursse ;

Who says I have
gone wrong ?
I should like to
sing you the
treble of a song,
if some one would
fill the quart.
Thank God, I am
very stiff in the
back,

and not worth
a pin.

Thocht I ane seruand lang haif bene,

My purchais is nocht worth ane preine;

156 I may sing Peblis on the greine,

For ocht that I may tursse.

Can you guess
my name?
I am Sandy
Solace,
son of Bess,
the wanton
from her
girlhood,

Quhat is my name, can ȝe not gesse?

Sirs, ken ȝe nocht Sandie Solace?

160 Thay callit my mother bonie Besse,

That dwelt betwene the bowis.

Of twelf ȝeir auld sho learnit to swyfe :

and of four or five

fathers,—no

joking,—one

after another.

Thankit be the great God on lyue,

164 Scho maid me fatheris four or fyue :

But dout, this is na mowis.

Quhen ane was deid, sho gat ane vther :

I had a power of

sires, lay and

cleric.

Was never man had sic ane mother.

168 Of fatheris sho maid me ane futher,

Of lawit men and leirit.

She is more than

a match for

twenty-four a

night, honour

bright.

Have you

seen the King?

I am his player;

and he is soon

coming here.

Long may

he reign!

Scho is baith wyse, worthie, and wicht;

For scho spairis nouther kuik nor knycht,

172 Ȝea, four and twentie on ane nicht,

And ay thair eine scho bleirit :

And, gif I lie, sirs, ȝe may speir.

Bot saw ye nocht the King cum heir?

176 I am ane sportour and playfeir

To that Royall ȝoung King.

He said he wald, within schort space,

Cum pas his tyme into this place.

180 I pray the Lord to send him grace,

That he lang tyme may ring.

PLACEBO.

Why so late?

Solace, quhy taryit ȝe sa lang?

SOLACE.

I could not come

any quicker; and

The feind a faster I micht gang :

184 I micht not thrist out throw the thrang

Of wyfes fyftein fidder.

12

Then for to rin I tuik ane rink ; *I ran away as*
Bot I felt neuer sik ane stink. *soon as I could.*
188 For our Lordis luif, gif me ane drink, *For God's love,*
    Placebo, my deir brother. *give me a drink.*

REX HVMANITAS.

My servant Solace, quhat gart ȝow tarie ? *Why did you delay ?*

SOLACE.

I wait not, sir, be sweit saint Marie : *I have been in*
192 I haue bene in ane feirie farie, *sad confusion.*
    Or ellis intill ane trance :
Sir, I haue sene, I ȝow assure, *I have seen the*
The fairest earthlie creature *lovellest creature*
196 That ever was formit be nature, *that ever was*
    And maist for to advance.
To luik on hir is great delyte, *created,*
With lippis reid and cheikis quhyte : *with red lips and*
200 I wald renunce all this warld quyte, *white cheeks,*
    For till stand in hir grace. *most desirable,*
Scho is wantoun, and scho is wyse *inviting,*
And cled scho is on the new gyse : *and dressed in*
204 It wald gar all ȝour flesche vpryse, *the new fashion.*
    To lüik vpon hir face. *Such a face !*
War I ane king, it sould be kend, *If I were a king,*
I sould not spair on hir to spend, *cost what it might, I would*
208 And this same nicht for hir to send, *send for her to*
    For my pleasure. *night.*
Quhat rak of ȝour prosperitie, *What is the*
Gif ȝe want Sensualitie ! *world worth*
212 I wald nocht gif ane sillie flie *without a*
    For ȝour treasure. *woman ?*

REX HVMANITAS.

Forsuith, my freinds, I think ȝe are not wyse *The King rebukes*
Till counsall me to break commandement, *Solace*

13

216 Directit be the Prince of Paradyce,—
Considering ʒe knaw that my intent
Is for till be to God obedient,—
Quhilk dois forbid men to be lecherous :
220 Do I nocht sa, perchance I will repent.
Thairfoir, I think ʒour counsall odious,
The quhilk ʒe gaif mee till ;
Becaus I haue bene, to this day,
224 Tanquam tabula rasa ;
That is als mekill as to say,
Redie for gude and ill.

for trying to tempt one who was minded to eschew lewdness, and repudiates his offer, as odious.

He had, hitherto, had no manner of experience whatever.

PLACEBO.

Beleiue ʒe that we will begyll ʒow,
228 Or from ʒour vertew we will wyle ʒow,
Or with euill counsall overseyll ʒow
Both into gude and euill ?
To tak ʒour graces part wee grant,
232 In all ʒour deidis participant,
Sa that ʒe be nocht ane ʒoung sanct,
And, syne, ane auld deuill.

Placebo says they have no wish to corrupt or mislead the King.

They will side with him, so that he be not a young saint and then an old devil.

WANTONNES.

Beleiue ʒe, Sir, that Lecherie be sin ?
236 Na, trow nocht that : this is my ressoun quhy :
First, at the Romane Kirk will ʒe begin,—
Quhilk is the lemand lamp of lechery,—
Quhair Cardinals and Bischops, generally,
240 To luif Ladies thay think ane pleasant sport,
And out of Rome hes baneist Chastity,
Quha with our Prelats can get na resort.

Wantonnes vouches the Romish Church, in proof that lechery is no sin. Chastity is banished out of Rome.

SOLACE.

Sir, quhill ʒe get ane prudent Queine,
244 I think ʒour Maiestie serein
Sould haue ane lustie Concubein,

Solace advises His Majesty to have a concubine,

To play ʒow withall.

For I knaw, be ʒour qualitie,

248   Ʒe want the gift of chastitie.

Fall to, in nomine Domini :

This is my counsall.

I speik, Sir, vnder protestatioun,

252   That nane at me haif indignatioun ;

For all the Prelats of this natioun,

For the maist part,

Thay think na schame to haue ane huir ;

256   And sum hes thrie vnder thair cuir.

This to be trew, Ile ʒow assuir,

    Ʒe sall heir efterwart.

Sir, knew [ʒe] all the mater throch,

260   To play ʒe wald begin.

Speir at the Monks of Bamirrinoch,

    Gif lecherie be sin.

for his comfort; as he lacks the gift of chastity.

For the prelates indulge, pretty generally, in concubinage; and some of them had a whole leash of mistresses. This is true; and do thou likewise. Ask the monks of Bamirrinoch if lechery is sin.

PLACEBO.

Sir, send ʒe for Sandie Solace,

264   Or ells ʒour monʒeoun Wantonnes ;

And pray my Ladie Priores ·

    The suith till declair,

Gif it be sin to tak Kaity,

268   Or to leif like ane bummillbaty.

The buik sayis Omnia probate,

    And nocht for to spair.

Placebo tells the King to ask the Prioress whether fornication is sin.

Prove all things.

SENSVALITIE.

Luifers, awalk ! behald the fyrie spheir!

272   Behauld the naturall dochter of Venus !

Behauld, luifers, this lustie Ladie cleir,

The fresche fonteine of Knichtis amorous,

Repleit with ioyis dulce and delicious :

276   Or quha wald mak to Venus observance ?

In my mirthfull chalmer melodious,

Lovers, look at me, Venus's daughter, lovely, full of joys. Pleasant is my bower to all. Thair sall thay find all pastyme and pleasance.

See my lovely Behauld my heid ! behauld my gay attyre !

neck, 280 Behauld my halse lusum and lilie quhite !

my glowing face, Behauld my visage flammand as the fyre !

my shapely breasts. Behauld my papis of portratour perfyte !

I please all To luke on mee luiffers hes greit delyte ;

kings, and, 284 Rycht sa hes all the Kingis of Christindome :

specially, the To thame I haif done pleasouris infinite,

Court of Rome. And, speciallie, vnto the Court of Rome.

My kiss is worth Ane kis of me war worth, in ane morning,

a million of gold; 288 A milȝioun of gold, to Knicht or King ;

and yet I readily And ȝit I am of nature sa towart,

give it to all. I lat no luiffer pas with ane sair hart.

My name is Of my name wald ȝe wit the veritie,

Sensuality. 292 Forsuith, thay call me Sensualitie.

Let us sing a I hauld it best, now, or we farther gang,

song to Venus. To Dame Venus let vs go sing ane sang.

HAMELINES.

Familiarity Madame, but tarying,

acquiesces 296 For to serue Venus deir,

We sall fall to and sing.

in this. Sister Danger, cum neir.

DANGER.

Danger Sister, I was nocht sweir

300 To Venus observance.

makes Howbeit I mak Dangeir,

ȝit, be continuance,

answer Men may haue thair pleasance ;

with 304 Thairfoir, let na man fray :

We will tak it, perchance,

hesitation. Howbeit that wee say nay.

HAMELINES.

Familiarity Sister, cum on ȝour way ;

16

308   And let vs nocht think lang,
    In all the haist wee may,
    To sing Venus ane sang.

*presses her
to sing a song
to Venus.*

DANGER.

    Sister, sing this sang I may not,
312 Without the help of gude Fund-Ionet.
    Fund-Ionet! hoaw! cum tak a part.

*Danger asks for
the help of
Fund-Jonet.*

FVND-IONET.

    That sall I do, with all my hart.
    Sister, howbeit that I am hais,
316 I am content to beir a bais.
    ʒe twa sould luif me as ʒour lyfe ;
    ʒe knaw I lernit ʒow baith to swyfe :
    In my chalmer—ʒe wait weill quhair—
320 Sen syne the feind ane man ʒe spair.

*Fund-Jonet,
though hoarse,
is ready to sing
bass.
She claims their
love, since she
initiated them.*

HAMELINES.

    Fund-Ionet, fy! ʒe ar to blame.
    To speik foull wordis think ʒe not schame

Objurgation.

FVND-IONET.

    Thair is ane hundreth heir sitand by,
324 That luifis geaping als weill as I,
    Micht thay get it in priuitie.
    Bot quha begins the sang, let se.

*Many a one
here is as wanton
as I.
But the song!*

REX HVMANITAS.

    Vp, Wantonnes! thow sleipis to lang.
328 Me thocht I hard ane mirrie sang :
    I the command in haist to gang
    Se quhat ʒon mirth may meine.

*The King tells
Wantonness to
see who is
singing.*

WANTONNES.

    I trow, Sir, be the Trinitie,

Sensuality, Sir,

I surmise,   332   ȝon same is Sensualitie :
whom I   Gif it be scho, sune sall I sie
would see.   That Soverance sereine.

REX HVMANITAS.

Who is it ?   Quhat war thay ȝon, to me declair.

WANTONNES.

Sensuality.   336   Dame Sensuall, baith gude and fair.

PLACEBO.

She can both   Sir, scho is mekill to avance ;
play and   For scho can baith play and dance,
dance.   That perfyt patron of plesance,
Her neck is like   340   Ane perle of pulchritude :
silk; her hair is   Soft as the silk is hir quhite lyre,
fine;   Hir hair is like the goldin wyre :
and I burn   My hart burnis in ane flame of fyre :
with passion.   344   I sweir ȝow, be the Rude.
She has not   I think scho is sa wonder fair,
her equal on   That in earth scho hes na compair.
earth.
If you knew   War ȝe weill leirnit at luffis lair,
love's lore, and
had once seen   348   And syne had hir anis sene,
her,   I wait, be cokis passioun,
you would give a   ȝe wald mak supplicatioun,
million for her   And spend on hir ane millioun,
love.   352   Hir lufe for till obteine.

SOLACE.

Shall she come to   Quhat say ȝe, sir ? ar ȝe content
you at once ?   That scho cum heir incontinent ?
What is the   Quhat vails ȝour kingdome and ȝour **rent,**
worth of power
and riches,   356   And all ȝour great treasure,
without joy   Without ȝe haif ane mirrie lyfe,
and quiet ?   And cast asyde all sturt and stryfe,
Till you get a   And, sa lang as ȝe want ane wyfe,
wife, take your
pleasure.   360   Fall to and tak ȝour pleasure ?

REX HVMANITAS.

Gif that be trew quhilk 3e me tell,
    I will not langer tarie,
Bot will gang preif that play, my sell,
364   Howbeit the warld me warie.
    Als fast as 3e may carie,
    Speid with all diligence :
    Bring Sensualitie,
368   Fra-hand, to my presence.
Forsuth, I wait not how it stands ;
Bot, sen I hard of 3our tythands,
My bodie trimblis, feit and hands,
372   And, quhiles, is hait as fyre.
I trow, Cupido with his dart
Hes woundit me out-throw the hart ;
My spreit will fra my bodie part,
376   Get I nocht my desyre.
Pas on away, with diligence,
And bring hir heir to my presence :
Spair nocht for trauell nor expence ;
380   I cair not for na cost.
Pas on 3our way, schone Wantonnes ;
And tak with 3ow Sandie Solace,
And bring that Ladie to this place,
384   Or els I am bot lost.
Commend me to that sweitest thing,
And present hir with this same Ring ;
And say I ly in languisching,
388   Except scho mak remeid.
With siching sair I am bot schent,
Without scho cum, incontinent,
My heauie langour to relent,
392   And saif me now fra deid.

WANTONNES.

Or 3e tuik skaith, be Gods goun,

The King yields, defying the world, and orders them to fetch Sensuality, at once, to him.

He finds himself very much excited.

Cupid's dart has pierced him; and he is very uneasy.

Let her come immediately, despite trouble and cost.

Wantonness and Solace are to bring Sensuality to him forthwith,

giving her a ring;

for he longs and sighs sorely for her to come and relieve his distress.

He is told he

shall
not be
disappointed.   396
Sensuality shall

come: but there

will be charges.   400

I leuer thair war not, vp nor doun,
Ane tume cunt into this toun,
　　Nor twentie myle about.
Doubt ȝe nocht, Sir, bot wee will get hir :
Wee sall be feirie for till fetch hir ;
Bot, faith ! wee wald speid all the better,
　　Till gar our pursses rout.

SOLACE.

Money is

indispensable ;

and we have   404

no ready coin.

Sir, let na sorrow in ȝow sink ;
Bot gif vs Ducats for till drink,
And wee sall never sleip ane wink,
　　Till it be back or eadge.
Ȝe ken weill, Sir, wee haue no cunȝe.

REX HVMANITAS.

The King
gives it,
and bids them   408
make haste.

Solace, sure that sall be no sunȝie :
Beir ȝe that bag vpon ȝour lunȝie.
　　Now, sirs, win weill ȝour wage :
I pray ȝow speid ȝow sone againe.

WANTONNES.

They promise

diligence,

whatever the   412

weather, and to

be back by mid-

night.   416

Ȝe ! of this sang, sir, wee ar faine :
Wee sall nother spair wind nor raine,
　　Till our days wark be done : ·
Fairweill ! for wee ar at the flicht.
Placebo, rewll our Roy at richt :
We sall be heir, man, or midnicht,
　　Thocht wee marche with the Mone.

WANTONNES.

Wantonness
greets Sensuality.

Pastyme, with pleasance & greit prosperitie,
Be to ȝow, Soveraine Sensualitie !

SENSVALITIE.

Whither ?

Sirs, ȝe ar welcum : quhair go ȝe? eist? or west?

20

WANTONNES.

420 In faith, I trow we be at the farrest.   "Farrest."

SENSVALITIE.

Quhat is ȝour name ? I pray ȝou, Sir, declair.   Your name?

WANTONNES.

Marie ! Wantonnes, the Kings secretair.   Wantonnes.

SENSVALITIE.

Quhat King is that quhilk hes sa gay a boy ?   From what king?

WANTONNES.

424 Humanitie, that richt redoutit Roy,   Humanity;
     Quhilk dois commend him to ȝow hartfullie,   and he sends you
     And sends ȝow heir ane ring with ane Rubie,   a ring, as a token
     In takin that, abuife all creatour,   that he
428 He hes chosen ȝow to be his Paramour.   has chosen you
     He bade me say that he will be bot deid,   as his paramour.
     Without that ȝe mak, haistelie, remeid.   Do not delay.

SENSVALITIE.

     How can I help him, althocht he suld forfair ?   How can I, no
432 ȝe ken, richt weill, I am na Medcinair.   physician, help
                                                        him ?

SOLACE.

     ȝes, lustie ladie, thocht he war never sa seik,   In a very natural
     I wait ȝe beare his health into ȝour breik.   way.
     Ane kis of ȝour sweit mow, in ane morning,   One kiss of yours
436 Till his seiknes micht be greit comforting.   will give him
                                                        great comfort.
     And, als, he maks ȝow supplicatioun,
     This nicht to mak with him collatioun.   Meet him
                                                        to-night.

SENSVALITIE.

     I thank his grace of his benevolence.   Sensuality agrees
440 Gude sirs, I sall be reddie, evin fra-hand :   to go at once;

2

21

In me thair sall be fund na negligence,

Baith nicht & day, quhen his grace will demand.

Pas ȝe befoir, and say I am cummand,

444 And thinks richt lang to haif of him ane sicht:

And I to Venus do mak ane faithfull band,

That in his arms I think to ly all nicht.

WANTONNES.

That salbe done: bot ȝit, or I hame pas,

448 Heir I protest for Hamelynes, ȝour las.

SENSVALITIE.

Scho salbe at command, sir, quhen ȝe will:

I traist scho sall find ȝow flinging ȝour fill.

WANTONNES.

Now hay! for ioy and mirth I dance.

452 Tak thair ane gay gamond of France:

Am I nocht worthie till avance,

That am sa gude a page,

And that sa spedelie can rin

456 To tyst my maister vnto sin?

The fiend a penny he will win

Of this his mariage.

I rew richt sair, be sanct Michell!

460 Nor I had pearst hir my awin sell;

For quhy ȝon King, be Bryds bell,

Kennis na mair of ane cunt

Nor dois the noueis of ane freir.

464 It war bot almis to pull my eir,

That wald not preif ȝon gallant geir.

Fy, that I am sa blunt!

I think, this day, to win greit thank.

468 Hay! as ane brydlit cat, I brank:

Alace! I haue wreistit my schank,

Yit gangis, be sanct Michaell!

Quhilk of my leggis, Sirs, as ӡe trow,

472 Was it that I did hurt evin now ?

Bot quhairto sould I speir at ӡow ?

I think thay baith ar haill.

Gude morrow, Maister, be the Mes !

one of his legs, but afterwards thinks they are both right.

REX HVMANITAS.

476 Welcum, my menӡeon, Wantonnes !

How hes thow sped in thy trauell ?

Welcome! What speed ?

WANTONNES.

Rycht weill, be him that herryit hell !

ӡour erand is weill done.

Very good.

REX HVMANITAS.

480 Then, Wantonnes, how weill is mee !

Thow hes deseruit baith meit and fie,

Be him that maid the Mone !

Thair is ane thing that I wald speir :

484 Quhat sall I do, quhen scho cums heir ?

For I knaw nocht the craft, perqueir,

Of luifers gyn :

Thairfoir, at lenth ӡe mon me leir

488 How to begin.

Then you deserve reward. But what shall I do when she comes ? For I am a novice in love-matters

WANTONNES.

To kis hir & clap hir, sir, be not affeard :

Sho will not schrink, thocht ӡe kis hir ane span

within the baird.

Gif ӡe think that sho thinks shame, then hyd *the*

bairns eine

492 With hir taill, & tent hir weil : ӡe wait quhat

I meine.

Will ӡe leif me, Sir, first for to go to ?

And I sall leirne ӡow all kewis how to do.

Kiss her, without fear of her resisting, &c., &c. Shall I go first, and show you ?

2 *

23

REX HVMANITAS.

By no
manner
of means.

496   God forbid, Wantonnes, that I gif the leife !
       Thou art ouer perillous ane page sic practiks to
       preife.

WANTONNES.

She comes.

Be wise.

Now, Sir, preife as ʒe pleis.   I se hir cumand.
Vse ʒour self grauelie : wee sall by ʒow stand.

SENSVALITIE.

Glory to thee,

Venus, for·

giving me such

beauty !

I will sacrifice

to thee.

All love me,—

clerics and

laymen,—

and all will, the

young especially.

None here could

truthfully deny

this.

I now go to a

powerful prince.

It delights me to

take him in

charge,—

O Queene Venus ! vnto thy Celsitude
500   I gif gloir, honour, laud, and reuerence,
       Quha grantit me sic perfite pulchritude,
       That Princes of my persone haue pleasance.
       I mak ane vow, with humbill obseruance,
504   Richt reuerentlie thy Tempill to visie,
       With sacrifice vnto thy Dyosie.
       Till everie stait I am so greabill,
       That few or nane refuses me, at all :
508   Paipis, Patriarks, or Prelats venerabill,
       Common pepill, and Princes temporall
       Ar subiect, all, to me, Dame Sensuall.
       Sa sall it be ay, quhill the warld indures,
512   And, speciallie, quhair ʒouthage hes the cures.
            Quha knawis the contrair ?
       I traist, few, in this companie,
       Wald thay declair the veritie,
516   How thay vse Sensualitie,
            Bot with me maks repair.
       And now my way I man auance
       Vnto ane Prince of great puissance,
520   Quhom ʒoung men hes in gouernance,
            Rolland into his rage.
       I am richt glaid, I ʒow assure,
       That potent Prince to get in cure,
524   Quhilk is of lustines the luir,

And greitest of curage.

a bold youth.

O potent Prince, of pulchritude preclair,

God Cupido preserue ʒour celsitude !

May Cupid and

528 And Dame Venus mot keip ʒour court fro cair,

Venus watch

As I wald sho suld keip my awin hart-blud !

over you !

REX HVMANITAS.

Welcum to me, peirles in pulchritude !

Welcome!

Welcum to me, thow sweiter nor the Lamber,

Take the lady

532 Quhilk hes maid me of all dolour denude !

Solace, convoy this Ladie to my chamber.

to my chamber.

SENSVALITIE.

I gang this gait with richt gude will.

I go willingly.

Sir Wantonnes, tarie ʒe stil ;

But do you two

536 And, Hamelines, the cap ʒeis fill,

And beir him cumpanie.

drink.

[HAMELINES.]

That sall I do, withoutin dout,

We will.

And he and I sall play cap'out.

WANTONNES.

540 Now, Ladie, len me that batye tout :

Fill up.

Fill in ; for I am dry.

Suppose we

ʒour dame, be this, trewlie,

Hes gotten vpon the gumis.

follow their

544 Quhat rak, thocht ʒe and I

Go iunne our iusting Lumis !

example ?

HAMELINES.

Content I am, with gude will,

I am nothing

Quhen euer ʒe ar reddie,

loth.

548 ʒour pleasure to fulfill.

WANTONNES.

Now, weill said, be our Ladie !

I will do as my

master, and just
Ile bair my Maister cumpanie,
Till that I may indure :
where we are,
552   Gif ȝe be quisland wantounlie,
on the floor.
We sall fling on the flure.

GVDE COVNSALL.

God save the
Immortall God, maist of magnificence,
Quhais Maiestie na Clark can comprehend,
hearers, and keep
556   Must saue ȝow all that giuis sic audience,
them from
And grant ȝow grace him never till offend,
offending Christ,
Quhilk on the Croce did willinglie ascend,
the Crucified !
And sched his pretious blude on everie side ;
May He rule and
560   Quhais pitious passioun from danger ȝow defend,
guide you !
And be ȝour gratious governour and gyde !
I come, because
Now, my gude freinds, considder, I ȝow beseik,
The caus maist principall of my cumming :
kings, without
564   Princis or Potestatis ar nocht worth ane leik,
me, are nothing.
Be thay not gydit be my gude gouerning.
To such
Thair was never Empriour, Conquerour, nor
    King,
my wisdom
Without my wisdome that micht thair wil
is all.
    avance.
But for me,
568   My name is Gude Counsall, without feinȝeing ;
Good Counsel,
Lords, for lack of my lair, ar brocht to mischance.
Finallie, for conclusioun,
confusion is
Quha halds me at delusioun
inevitable.
572   Sall be brocht to confusioun :
    And this I vnderstand ;
I have dwelt
For I haue maid my residence
With hie Princes of greit puissance,
in many
576   In Ingland, Italie, and France,
a land,
    And monie vther Land.
but have long
Bot out of Scotland—wa ! alace !—
I haif bene fleimit lang tyme space :
been banished
580   That garris our gyders all want grace,
Scotland ;
    And die befoir thair day.

Becaus thay lychtlyit Gude Counsall,

Fortune turnit on thame hir saill,

584 Quhilk brocht this Realme to meikill baill.

Quha can the contrair say ?

My Lords, I came nocht heir to lie.

Wa is me ; for King Humanitie

588 Overset with Sensualitie,

In th' entrie of his ring,

Throw vicious counsell insolent.

Sa thay may get riches or rent,

592 To his weilfair thay tak na tent,

Nor quhat sal be th' ending.

Ʒit in this Realme I· wald mak sum repair,

Gif I beleifit my name suld nocht forfair ;

596 For, wald this King be gydit ʒit with resioun,

And on misdoars mak punitioun,

Howbeit I haif lang tyme bene exyllit,

I traist in God my name suld ʒit be styilit :

600 Sa, till I se God send mair of his grace,

I purpois till repois me in this place.

FLATTERIE.

Mak roume, sirs, hoaw ! that I may rin !

Lo, se quhair I am new cum,

604 Begaryit all with sindrie hewis !

Let be ʒour din, till I begin,

And I sall schaw ʒow of my newis.

Throuchout all Christindome I haue past,

608 And am cum heir now, at the last,

Tostit on sea ay sen Ʒuill day,

That wee war faine to hew our Mast,

Nocht half ane myle beʒond the May.

612 Bot now amang ʒow I will remaine :

I purpois never to sail againe,

To put my lyfe in chance of watter.

Was never sene sic wind and raine,

Right margin glosses:

whence

manifold

misfortune.

I come, for that

King Humanity,

at the outset of

his reign, is

misguided by

vicious and

greedy

counsellors,

heedless of

consequences.

May the king

still be guided by

reason ; and may

I regain my

honour here.

Hence I mean to

stay awhile.

Room!

Look at my

bravery, and

hear my news.

A traveller, I

come, sea-tossed

since last

Christmas.

No more of sea

for me, nor its

risks and

storms!

There was such	616	Nor of Schipmen sic clitter clatter.

There was such a gale, and din of voices,
616 Nor of Schipmen sic clitter clatter.
Sum bade haill ! and sum bade standby !
On steirburd ! hoaw ! aluiff ! fy ! fy !

rattling of ropes,
Quhill all the raipis beguith to rattil.
620 Was never Roy sa fleyd as I,

flapping and
Quhen all the sails playd brittill brattill.

rending of sails;
To se the waws, it was ane wonder,
And wind, that raif the sails in sunder.

and I was in a
624 Bot I lay braikand like ane Brok,

sad plight
And shot sa fast, aboue and vnder,

therefrom.
The Deuill durst not cum neir my dok.

Escaped,
Now am I scapit fra that effray :

I am gay.
628 Quhat say ʒe, sirs ? am I nocht gay ?

I am the same
Se ʒe not Flatterie, ʒour awin fuill,

that was with
That ʒeid to mak this new array ?

you at Christmas.
Was I not heir with ʒow at ʒuill ?
632 ʒes, be my faith, I think on weill.

Where are my
Quhair ar my fallows that wald nocht fail ?

mates ?
We suld haue cum heir for ane cast.

Falsehood !
Hoaw ! Falset, hoaw !

FALSET.

Who calls me ?
636 Wa fair the Deuill ?
Quha is that that cryis for me sa fast ?

FLATTERIE.

Don't you know me, brother ?
Quhy, Falset, brother, knawis thou not me ?
Am I nocht thy brother Flattrie ?

FALSET.

Welcome !
640 Now welcome, be the Trinitie !
This meitting cums for gude.

Let us embrace,
Now let me breste the in my armis :

as we love.
Quhen freinds meits, harts warmis,
644 Quod Iok, that frelie fude.

How here ?
How happinit ʒow into this place ?

28

FLATTERIE.

Now, be my saul! evin on a cace :

I come in sleipand at the port,

648   Or ever I wist, amang this sort.

Quhair is Dissait, that limmer loun?

Quite by way of chance.

Where is Deceit?

FALSET.

I left him drinkand in the toun :

He will be heir incontinent.

Drinking. He will be here soon.

FLATTERIE.

652   Now, be the haly Sacrament !

Thay tydingis comforts all my hart.

I wait, Dissait will tak my part :

He is richt craftie, as ʒe ken,

656   And counsallour to the Merchand-men.

Let vs ly doun heir, baith, and spy

Gif wee persaue him cummand by.

I am glad of it.

He is a shrewd one, you know.

Let us watch for him.

DISSAIT.

Stand by the gait, that I may steir.

660   Aisay ! Koks bons ! how cam I heir?

I can not mis to tak sum feir,

    Into sa greit ane thrang.

Marie ! heir ane cumlie congregatioun !

664   Quhat ! ar ʒe, sirs, all of ane natioun?

Maisters, I speik be protestatioun,

    In dreid ʒe tak me wrang.

Ken ʒe not, sirs, quhat is my name?

668   Gude faith ! I dar not schaw it, for schame.

Sen I was clekit of my Dame,

    ʒit was I never leill :

For Katie Vnsell was my mother,

672   And common theif my father-brother :

Of sic freindship I had ane fither;

    Howbeit, I can not steill :

Help me steer.

How came I here? I am frightened.

Are you all of one nation?

Excuse me.

I do not dare to tell my name, from shame.

Kitty Bad-un was my mother; a thief, my father. Yet I cannot steal.

But I am ready

to borrow

and lend,

and to fight.

I live among
merchants.
My name?

I am Deceit.

I am with you

any way.

I met Good

Counsel,—

Devil take him!

Bot ʒit I will borrow and len,
676 As, be my cleathing, ʒe may ken
That I am cum of nobill men;
     And, als, I will debait
That querrell with my feit and hands.
680 And I dwell amang the merchands :
My name gif onie man demands,
     Thay call me Dissait.
Bon-iour ! brother, with all my hart.
684 Heir am I cum to tak ʒour part,
     Baith into gude and euill.
I met Gude Counsall be the way,
Quha pat me in ane felloun fray :
688 I gif him to the Deuill.

                              FALSET.

How did you get
away ?

How chaipit ʒe, I pray ʒow tell.

                              DISSAIT.

I slipped into a

brothel, and there

hid myself and

had adventures.

Why came you
here ?

I slipit into ane·bordell,
     And hid me in ane bawburds bed :
692 Bot suddenlie hir schankis I sched,
     With hoch hurland amang hir howis :
God wait gif wee maid monie mowis.
How came ʒe heir, I pray ʒow tell me.

                              FALSET.

To seek King
Humanity.

696 Marie ! to seik King Humanitie.

                              DISSAIT.

And so I,

too.

Let us devise

some cunning

scheme.

Now, be the gude Ladie that me bair !
That samin hors is my awin Mair.
Now with our purpois let vs mell :
700 Quhat is ʒour counsall, I pray ʒow tell.
Sen we thrie seiks ʒon nobill King,
Let vs deuyse sum subtill thing.

30

And, als, I pray ȝow, as my brother,   Let us be

704　That we, ilk ane, be trew to vther.   mutually true.

I mak ane vow, with all my hart,   I will aid you,

In gude and euill to tak ȝour part.

I pray to God, nor I be hangit,   and will not play

708　Bot I sall die, or ȝe be wrangit.   you false.

FALSET.

Quhat is thy counsall that wee do ?   My advice is,

Marie ! sirs, this is my counsall, lo !

Till tak our tyme, quhill wee may get it ;   that we set to

712　For now thair is na man to let it.   work at once.

Fra tyme the King begin to steir him,   We must keep

Marie ! Gude Counsall I dreid cum neir him ;

And, be wee knawin with Correctioun,   Good Counsel

716　It will be our confusioun.   away.

Thairfoir, my deir brother, deuyse   What deceit shall

To find sum toy of the new gyse.   we use ?

FLATTERIE.

Marie ! I sall finde ane thousand wyles :   Let us disguise

720　Wee man turne our claithis, & change our stiles,

And disagyse vs, that na man ken vs.   ourselves as

Hes na man Clarkis cleathing to len vs ?   clerks, just come

And let vs keip graue countenance,

724　As wee war new cum out of France.   from France.

DISSAIT.

Now, be my saull ! that is weill deuysit.   Well thought !

ȝe sall se me sone disagysit.   I will soon disguise myself.

FALSET.

And sa sall I, man, be the Rude !   And I, too.

728　Now, sum gude fallow len me ane hude.   Lend me a hood.

DISSAIT.

Now am I buskit, and quha can spy—   Who could say

this was myself?

    The Deuill stik me !—gif this be I ?

I really am not

    If this be I, or not, I can not weill say.

sure it is.

732   Or hes the Feind or Farie-folk borne me away

FALSET.

With the addition
of a coif, I should
be quite
disguised.

    And, gif my hair war vp in ane how,
    The feind ane man wald ken me, I trow.
    Quhat sayis thou of my gay garmoun ?

DISSAIT.

What do you
mean to make
yourself,
Flattery ?

736   I say thou luiks euin like ane loun.
    Now, brother Flatterie, quhat do ʒe ?
    Quhat kynde of man schaip ʒe to be ?

FLATTERIE.

    Now, be my faith ! my brother deir,

A friar.

740   I will gang counterfit the Freir.

DISSAIT.

You cannot
preach.

    A Freir ! quhairto ? ʒe can not preiche.

FLATTERIE.

I can flatter.

    Quhat rak, man ! I can richt weill fleich.

I may become

    Perchance Ile cum [till] that honour

King's confessor.

744   To be the Kings confessour.

Friars are

    Pure Freirs are free at any feast,

favoured.

    And marchellit, ay, amang the best.

Bishops depute

    Als, God to them hes lent sic graces,

748   That Bischops puts them in thair places,

them to preach ;

    Out-throw thair Dioceis to preiche :

and yet they

    Bot ferlie nocht, howbeit thay fleich ;

differ from

    For, schaw thay all the veritie,

Bishops.

752   Thaill want the Bischops charitie.

They never

    And, thocht the corne war never sa skant,

starve ;

    The gudewyfis will not let Freirs want ;

and goodwives

    For quhy thay ar thair confessours,

side with them,

756   Thair heauinlie prudent counsalours :

.Thairfoir the wyfis plainlie taks thair parts,
And shawis the secreits of thair harts
To Freirs, with better will, I trow,
760 Nor thay do to thair bed-fallow.

and are more open to them than to their own husbands.

DISSAIT.

And I reft, anis, ane Freirs coull,
Betuix Sanct Iohnestoun and Kinnoull.
I sall gang fetch it, gif ȝe will tarie.

I will fetch a friar's cowl I once came by.

FLATTERIE.

764 Now play me that of companarie :
Ȝe saw him nocht, this hundreth ȝeir,
That better can counterfeit tħe Freir.

I never saw a friar counterfeited better.

DISSAIT.

Heir is thy gaining, all and sum :
768 This is ane koull of Tullilum.

Here is the cowl.

FLATTERIE.

Quha hes ane portouns for to len me ?
The feind ane saull, I trow, will ken me.

Who has a breviary to lend me ?

FALSET.

Now gang thy way, quhair euer thow will ;
772 Thow may be fallow to freir Gill :
Bot with Correctioun gif wee be kend,
I dreid wee mak ane schamefull end.

Now you will do. Woe to us, if found out !

FLATTERIE.

For that mater, I dreid na thing :
776 Freiris ar exemptit fra the King ;
And Freiris will reddie entries get,
Quhen Lords ar haldin at the ȝet.

Have no fear. Friars are always admitted.

FALSET.

Wee man do mair ȝit, be Sanct Iames !

Now let us

change our
names.

780 For wee mon, all thrie, change our names.
     Hayif me, and I sall baptize thee.

DISSAIT.

What will you
call me?

Be God! and thair-about may it be.
How will thou call me, I pray the tell.

FALSET.

Or myself?

784 I wait not how to call my sell.

DISSAIT.

Name him.

Bot зit anis name the bairns name.

FALSET.

Discretion, then.

Discretioun, Discretioun, in Gods name.

DISSAIT.

My compaternal
present?

I neid nocht now to cair for thrift :
788 Bot quhat salbe my Godbairne gift ?

FALSET.

All the devils in
hell.

I gif зow all the Deuilis of hell.

DISSAIT.

Keep them.
I baptize you.
Your name?

Na, brother ; hauld that to thy sell.
Now sit doun ; let me baptize the :
792 I wait not quhat thy name sould be.

FALSET.

Name him.

Bot зit anis name the bairns name.

DISSAIT.

Sapience.

Sapience, in ane warlds-schame.

FLATTERIE.

Baptize me.

Brother Dissait, cum baptize me.

DISSAIT.

Then kneel.

796 Then sit doun lawlie on thy kne.

34

FLATTERIE.

Now, brother, name the bairns name.   *Name him.*

DISSAIT.

Devotioun, the Deuillis name.   *Devotion.*

FLATTERIE.

The deuill resaue the lurdoun loun !   *You have wetted*
800   Thow hes wet all my new schawin croun.   *all my tonsure.*

DISSAIT.

Devotioun, Sapience, and Discretioun,   *Now we can*
   Wee thre may rewll this Regioun.   *control this*
   Wee sall find monie craftie things   *realm,*
804   For to begyll ane hundreth Kingis :   *what between*
   For thow can richt weil crak and clatter ;   *vapouring,*
   And I sall feinʒe ; and thow sall flatter.   *feigning, and flattering.*

FLATTERIE.

Bot I wald haue, or wee depairtit,   *Let us take a*
808   Ane drink, to mak vs better hartit.   *drink.*

(*Now the King sall cum fra his chamber.*)

DISSAIT.

Weill said, be him that herryit hell !   *So I was*
   I was euin thinkand that, my sell.   *thinking.*
   Now, till wee get the Kings presence,   *Now let us keep*
812   Wee will sit doun and keip silence.   *quiet.*
   I se ane ʒeoman : quhat ever be,   *I see the King*
   Ile wod my lyfe, ʒon same is he.   *coming.*
   Feir nocht, brother ; bot hauld ʒow still,   *Let us learn his*
816   Till wee haue hard quhat is his will.   *will.*

REX HVMANITAS.

Now, quhair is Placebo and Solace ?   *Where are my*
   Quhair is my minʒeoun, Wantonnes ?   *three friends !*
   Wantonnes ! hoaw ! cum to me sone !   *Wantonnes !*

WANTONNES.

I had not done.   820   Quhy cryit ȝe, sir, till I had done?

REX HVMANITAS.

What were you doing?   Quhat was ȝe doand? tell me that.

WANTONNES.

Learning a lesson, with amazement.
Mary! leirand how my father me gat.
I wait nocht how it stands, but doubt:
824   Me think the warld rinnis round about.

REX HVMANITAS.

I was in the same way.
And sa think I, man: be my thrift!
I se fyfteine Mones in the lift.

HAMELINES.

You are content?   Gat ȝe nocht that quhilk ȝe desyrit?
And tired.   828   Sir, I beleif that ȝe ar tyrit.

DANGER.

I kept Placebo and Solace merry.
Bot, as for Placebo and Solace,
I held them baith in mirrines.

SOLACE.

Sir, are you pleased?
Now schaw me, sir, I ȝow exhort,
832   How ar ȝe of ȝour luif content.
Did you like it?   Think ȝe not this ane mirrie sport?

REX HVMANITAS.

Very well.   ȝea, that I do, in verament.
Who are they   Quhat bairnis ar ȝon vpon the bent?
yonder?   836   I did nocht se them all this day.

WANTONNES.

When they come up, listen to them.
Thay will be heir incontinent.
Stand still, and heir quhat thay will say.

(*Now the vycis cums, and maks salutatioun, saying :*)

DISSAIT.

840 Laud, honor, gloir, triumph, & victory   We salute the
Be to ʒour maist excellent Maiestie!   King.

REX HVMANITAS.

ʒe ar welcum, gude freinds, be the Rude!   You are welcome.
Appeirandlie, ʒe seime sum men of gude.   What are your
Quhat ar ʒour names, tell me without delay.   names?

DISSAIT.

844 Discretioun, Sir, is my name, perfay.   Discretion.

REX HVMANITAS.

Quhat is ʒour name, sir, with the clipit croun?   Yours?

FLATTRIE.

But dout, my name is callit Devotioun.   Devotion.

REX HVMANITAS.

Welcum, Devotioun, be Sanct Iame!   Welcome.
848 Now, sirray, tell quhat is ʒour name.   And yours?

FALSET.

Marie! sir, thay call me :—quhat call thay me?   My name?

REX HVMANITAS.

Can ye nocht tell quhat is ʒour name?   Don't you know it?

FALSET.

I kend it quhen I cam fra hame.   I knew it just now.

REX HVMANITAS.

852 Quhat gars ʒe can nocht schaw it now?   Why cannot you tell it?

FALSET.

Marie! thay call me thin drink, I trow!   Thin drink.

REX HVMANITAS.

Thin drink! quhat kynde of name is that?   What a name!

3

37

DISSAIT.

Sapiens, thou seruis to beir ane plat.

Sapiens, you are stupid.

856 Me think thow schawis the not weill-wittit.

FALSET.

Yes: Sypiens.

Sypeins, sir, sypeins : marie ! now ze hit it.

FLATTRIE.

His name is Sapientia.

Sir, gif ze pleis to let him say,
His name is Sapientia.

FALSET.

So it is.

860 That same is it, be Sanct Michell.

REX HVMANITAS.

Why could not you say so, yourself ?

Quhy could thou not tell it thy sell?

FALSET.

Pardon me. From plethora of sapience sometimes I am entranced.

I was up above Trinity.

I pray zour grace appardoun me,
And I sall schaw the veritie.
864 I am sa full of Sapience,
That, sumtyme, I will tak ane trance :
My spreit wes reft fra my bodie,
Now heich abone the Trinitie.

REX HVMANITAS.

Sapience should be a likely person.

868 Sapience suld be ane man of gude.

FALSET.

You may believe so.

Sir, ze may ken that, be my hude !

REX HVMANITAS.

With Sapience, Discretion, and Devotion, I can now rule aright, and have them for my secretary,

Now haue I Sapience and Discretioun,
How can I faill to rewll this Regioun ?
872 And Devotioun, to be my confessour :
Thir thrie came in ane happie hour.
Heir I mak the my secretar ;

And thou salbe my thesaurar;
876 And thow salbe my counsallour
In sprituall things, and confessour.

treasurer, and counsellor and confessor.

FLATTRIE.

I sweir to ʒow, sir, be sanct Ann!
ʒe met never with ane wyser man ;
880 For monie a craft, sir, do I can,
War thay weill knawin.
Sir, I haue na feill of flattrie,
Bot fosterit with Philsophie ;
884 Ane strange man in Astronomie,
Quhilk salbe schawin.

You have, in me, one of the wisest and most learned of men. No flatterer, I am an adept in philosophy and astronomy.

FALSET.

And I haue greit intelligence
In quelling of the quintessence.
888 Bot, to preif my experience,
Sir, len me fourtie crownes,
To mak multiplicatioun ;
And tak my obligatioun :
892 Gif wee mak fals narratioun,
Hauld vs for verie lownes.

As for me, I know all about the quintessence. Lend me forty crowns; and, if we deceive you, count us villains.

DISSAIT.

Sir, I ken, be ʒour Physnomie,
ʒe sall conqueis, or els I lie,
896 Danskin, Denmark, and Almane,
Spittelfeild, and the Realme of Spane :
ʒe sall haue at ʒour governance
Ranfrow and all the Realme of France ;
900 ʒea, Rugland, and the toun of Rome,
Castorphine, and al christindome :
Quhairto, sir, be the Trinitie !
ʒe ar ane verie Apersie.

I know, by your physiognomy, that you are destined to conquer many realms and regions,—all Christendom. You are a very A per se.

FLATTRIE.

I have learned
palmistry.
Show me your
hand, to tell your
fortune, bad or
good.
You will have 15
queens and 300
concubines.
What a white
face,—and arms,
hands, legs!
You could knock
down 1500.

904   Sir, quhen I dwelt in Italie,
      I leirit the craft of Palmistrie.
      Schaw me the lufe, Sir, of ȝour hand,
      And I sall gar ȝow vnderstand
908   Gif ȝour grace be infortunat,
      Or gif ȝe be predestinat.
      I see ȝe will haue fyfteine Queenes
      And fyfteine scoir of Concubeines.
912   The Virgin Marie saife ȝour grace !
      Saw ever man sa quhyte ane face,
      Sa greit ane arme, sa fair ane hand !
      Thairs nocht sic ane leg in al this land.
916   War ȝe in armis, I think na wonder,
      Howbeit ȝe dang doune fyfteine hunder.

DISSAIT.

And how he fits
his clothes!
No man is fitter
for a king.

      Now, be my saull ! thats trew thow sayis :
      Wes never man set sa weill his clais.
920   Thair is na man in Christintie,
      Sa meit to be ane King as ȝe.

FALSET.

You should thank
the Trinity, sir,
for sending us
three to you.

      Sir, thank the haly Trinitie,
      That send vs to ȝour cumpanie.
924   For God ! nor I gaip in ane gallows,
      Gif ever ȝe fand thrie better fallows.

REX HVMANITAS.

Welcome !

      ȝe ar richt welcum, be the Rude !
      ȝe seime to be thrie men of gude.

      (Heir sall Gude Counsall schaw himself in the feild.)

Who is that
yonder?
Bring him, if he
wishes to come to
me.

928   Bot quha is ȝon that stands sa still ?
      Ga spy, and speir quhat is his will ;
      And, gif he ȝearnis my presence,
      Bring him to mee with Diligence.

DISSAIT.

932 That sall wee do, be Gods breid !
We 's bring him eather quick or deid.

We will do as
you bid.

REX HVMANITAS.

I will sit still heir and repois.
Speid ȝow agane to me, my Iois.

Go, while I sit
here.

FALSET.

936 Ȝe, hartlie, Sir : keip ȝow in clois
And quyet, till wee cum againe.
Brother, I trow, be coks toes !
Ȝon bairdit bogill cums fra ane traine.

Meantime, keep
quiet.
But I fear
mischief.

DISSAIT.

940 Gif he dois sa, he salbe slaine.
I doubt him nocht, nor ȝit ane vther.
Trowit I that he come for ane traine,
Of my freindis I sould rais ane futher.

I will prevent
that, fearlessly.
I would raise my
friends.

FLATTRIE.

944 I doubt full sair, be God him sell !
That ȝon auld churle be Gude Counsell.
Get he anis to the Kings presence,
We thrie will get na audience.

I fear it is Good
Counsel.
He must not get
near the King.

DISSAIT.

948 That matter I sall tak on hand,
And say, it is the Kings command,
That he anone devoyd this place,
And cum nocht neir the Kings grace,—
952 And that, vnder the paine of tressoun.

I will undertake
to say he must be
off at once, under
pain of treason.

FLATTRIE.

Brother, I hauld ȝour counsell ressoun.
Now let vs heir quhat he will say.
Auld lyart beard, gude day ! gude day !

Well thought !
What says he ?
Good morrow !

41

GVDE COVNSALL.

Good morrow!   956   Gude day, againe! sirs, be the rude!
The Lord better   The Lord mot mak ȝow men of gude!
you!

DISSAIT.

We need no   Pray nocht for vs to Lord nor Ladie;
prayers, being
good already.   For we ar men of gude alreadie.
Your name?   960   Sir, schaw to vs quhat is ȝour name.

GVDE COVNSALL.

Good Counsel.   Gude Counsell thay call me at hame.

FALSET.

Is it so?   Quhat says thow, carle? ar thow Gude Counsell?
Away, then!   Swyith! pak the sone, vnhappie vnsell!
And stay away, 964   Gif ever thou cum this gait againe,
or we will slay
you.   I vow to God, thou sall be slaine.

GVDE COVNSALL.

Only let me speak   I pray ȝow, sirs, gif me licence
two words to the   To cum anis to the Kings presence,
King.   968   To speik bot twa words to his grace.

FLATTRIE.

Away!   Swyith! hursone carle: devoyd this place!

GVDE COVNSALL.

I know you well   Brother, I ken ȝow weill aneuch,
enough. You are   Howbeit ȝe mak it never sa teuch:—
Flattery, Deceit, 972 Flattrie, Dissait, and Fals Report,
and False Report,
keeping me from   That will not suffer to resort
the King.   Gude Counsall to the Kings presence.

DISSAIT.

Be off!   Suyith! hursun carle: gang, pak the hence!
Come again, and 976   Gif ever thou cum this gait agane,
be killed.   I vow to God, thou sall be slane.

42

(Heir sall thay hurle away Gude Counsall.)   Good Counsel
                                                  is turned away.
[GVDE COVNSALL.]

Sen, at this tyme, I can get na presence,   I have no remedy
Is na remeid bot tak in patience.   but patience.
980 Howbeit Gude Counsall haistelie be nocht hard   Though Good
     With ȝoung Princes, ȝit sould thay noch be skard; Counsel is not at
                                                        first heard by
     Bot, quhen ȝouthheid hes blawin his wanton   young Princes,
          blast,   he rules them,
                                                     finally, when
     Then sall Gude Counsall rewll him, at the last. youth is past.

(Now the Vycis gangs to ane counsall.)

FLATTRIE.

984 Now, quhill Gude Counsall is absent,   Now that Good
     Brother, wee mon be diligent,   Counsel is not
     And mak, betwix vs, sikker bands,   here, we must
                                                      agree to help each
     Quhen vacands fallis in onie Lands,   other, when good
988 That everie man help weill his fallow.   luck falls.

DISSAIT.

I had, deir brother, be Alhallow!   Only do not
Sa ȝe fische nocht within our bounds.   poach.

FLATTRIE.

That sall I nocht, be Gods wounds!   You may depend
992 Bot I sall plainlie tak ȝour partis.   on me.

FALSET.

Sa sall wee thyne, with all our hartis.   Let us lose
Bot haist vs, quhill the King is ȝoung;   no time;
Let everie man keip weill ane toung,   observing
996 And, in ilk quarter, haue ane spy,   secrecy, and
     Vs till adverteis haistelly,   employing spies
     Quhen ony casualities   to warn us of
     Sall happin into our countries :   casualties,
1000 And let vs mak provisioun,   while he is
     Or he cum to discretioun.   still heedless.
     Na mair he waits, now, nor ane sant,   At present, he

takes no thought.
Quhat thing it is to haif or want.

All must be done 1004 Or he cum till his perfyte age,

before he comes
We sall be sikker of our wage :

of age.
And then let everie carle craif vther.

DISSAIT.

You are a
That mouth speik mair, my awin deir brother.

cunning 1008 For God! nor I rax in ane raip,

counsellor.
Thow may gif counsall to the Paip.

(Now thay returne to the King.)

REX HVMANITAS.

Why were you
Quhat gart ʒou bid sa lang fra my presence ?

so long away ?
I think it lang since ʒe depairtit thence.

Who was he 1012 Quhat man was ʒon, with an greit bostous beird?

of the beard ?
Me thocht he maid ʒow, all thrie, very feard.

DISSAIT.

A burglar,
It was ane laidlie lurdan loun,

Cumde to break buithis into this toun.

whom we have 1016 Wee haue gart bind him with ane poill,

disposed of.
And send him to the theifis hoill.

REX HVMANITAS.

Take we our
Let him sit thair, with ane mischance ;

pleasure.
And let vs go to our pastance.

WANTONNES.

Let us play some 1020 Better go reuell at the rackat,

Or ellis go to the hurlie hackat,

game, or have
Or, then, to schaw our curtlie corsses,

a horse-race.
Ga se quha best can rin thair horsses.

SOLACE.

Let Sensuality 1024 Na, soveraine, or wee farther gang,

sing a song.
Gar Sensualitie sing ane sang.

(Heir sall the Ladies sing ane sang, the King sall ly doun amang
the Ladies, and then Veritie sall enter.)

VERITIE.

Diligite Iustitiam qui iudicatis terram.

Luif Iustice, ȝe quha hes ane Iudges cure
1028 In earth, and dreid the awfull Iudgement
- Of him that sall cum iudge baith rich and pure,
'. Rycht terribilly, with bludy wounds rent.
That dreidfull day into ȝour harts imprent;
1032 Beleuand weill, how and quhat maner ȝe
Vse Iustice heir, til vthers, thair, at lenth,
That day, but doubt, sa sall ȝe iudgit be.
Wa, than, and duill be to ȝow Princes, all,
1036 Sufferand the pure anes for till be opprest!
In everlasting burnand fyre ȝe sall
With Lucifer richt dulfullie be drest.
Thairfoir, in tyme for till eschaip that nest,
1040 Feir God, do law and Iustice equally
Till everie man; se that na puir opprest
Vp to the hevin on ȝow ane vengence cry.
Be iust iudges, without fauour or fead;
1044 And hauld the Ballance euin till everie wicht.
Let not the fault be left into the head,
Then sall the members reulit be at richt;
For quhy subiects do follow, day and nicht, .
1048 Thair governours, in vertew and in vyce.
Ȝe ar the lamps that sould schaw them the licht
To leid them on this sliddrie rone of yce.
Mobile mutatur semper cum principe vulgus.
1052 And, gif ȝe wald ȝour subiectis war weill geuin,
Then verteouslie begin the dance, ȝour sell;
Going befoir, then they anone, I wein,
Sall follow ȝow, eyther till heuin or hell.
1056 Kings sould of gude exempils be the well;
Bot, gif that ȝour strands be intoxicate,
In steid of wyne, thay drink the poyson fell:
Thus pepill follows, ay, thair principate.

Love justice, ye judges, holding in dread the Judgment.

As you have judged others, so shall you be judged, yourselves.

Woe to oppressors, reserved for burning!

Then fear God, do justice, and prevent the cry to Heaven for vengeance on you.

Eschew partiality.

Set an example of virtue, and your subjects will imitate it.

Ye are to light their way.

According to your guidance the people will follow, either to Heaven or to Hell.

Beware that, instead of wine, you give them not drink of poison.

And do you,	1060	Sic luceat lux vestra coram hominibus, vt vi-
Prelates, look to		deant opera vestra bona.
it that your		And, specially, ȝe Princes of the Preists,
lights so shine as		That of peopill hes spiritual cuir,
to advantage the		Dayly ȝe sould revolue into ȝour breistis,
lay folk.	1064	How that thir haly words ar still maist sure.
Lead godly lives,		In verteous lyfe gif that ȝe do indure,
and the people		The pepill wil tak mair tent to ȝour deids
will copy you		
alike in your		Then to ȝour words, and, als, baith rich and puir
works and words.	1068	Will follow ȝow baith in ȝour warks and words.

(Heir sal Flattrie spy Veritie with ane dum countenance.)

My name is		Gif men of me wald haue intelligence,
Truth.		Or knaw my name, thay call me Veritie.
I have had much		Of Christis law I haue experience,
experience.	1072	And hes over-saillit many stormie sey.
I am in quest of		Now am I seikand King Humanitie ;
King Humanity,		For of his grace I haue gude esperance,
whom I hope to		
benefit, when		Fra tyme that he acquaintit be with mee,
once he knows		
me	1076	His honour and heich gloir I sall avance.

(Heir sall Veritie pas to hir sait.)

DISSAIT.

Good morrow !	Gude day, father : quhair haue ȝe bene ?
What news ?	Declair till vs of ȝour nouels.

FLATTRIE.

There is Lady		Thair is now lichtit on the grene,
Truth.	1080	Dame Veritie, be Buiks and bels !
If she gets at the		Bot cum scho to the Kings presence,
King, there is no		
peace for us.		Thair is na buit for vs to byde :
Let us be off.		Thairfoir, I red vs all go hence.

FALSET.

Not so.	1084	That will we nocht ȝit, be Sanct Bryde !
Rather, let us		Bot wee sall ather gang or ryde

To Lords of Spritualitie,

And gar them trow, ȝou bag of pryde

1088 Hes spokin manifest heresie.

(Heir thay cum to the Spritualitie.)

FLATTRIE.

O reverent fatheris of the Sprituall stait,

Wee counsall ȝow, be wyse and vigilant.

Dame Veritie hes lychtit, now of lait,

1092 And in hir hand beirand the Newtestament.

Be scho ressauit, but doubt wee ar bot schent :

Let hir nocht ludge, thairfoir, into this Land.

And this wee reid ȝow do incontinent,

1096 Now quhill the King is with his luif sleipand.

SPRITVALITIE.

Wee thank ȝow, freinds, of ȝour benevolence :

It sall be done, evin as ȝe haue devysit.

Wee think ȝe serue ane gudlie recompence,

1100 Defendand vs, that wee be nocht supprysit.

In this mater wee man be weill aduysit,

Now quhill the King misknawis the veritie.

Be scho ressauit, then wee will be deprysit.

1104 Quhat is ȝour counsell, brother, now let se.

ABBOT.

I hauld it best, that wee, incontinent,

Gar hauld hir fast into Captivitie,

Vnto the thrid day of the Parlament,

1108 And then accuse hir of hir herisie,

Or than banische hir out of this cuntrie ;

For, with the King gif Veritie be knawin,

Of our greit gloir wee will degradit be,

1112 And all our secreits to the commouns schawin.

PERSONE.

Ȝe se the King is ȝit effeminate,

Side notes:

go and lay a charge of heresy against her.

We come to report of Lady Truth, who has appeared, bearing the New Testament.

She must not be received, but must be expelled from the land, and that while the King still sleeps.

It shall be even so ; and you deserve well of us. We must be cautious. Her success would be our ruin.

Let her be cast into bonds, and accused of heresy, or banished. If the King comes to know her, we shall be degraded and exposed.

The King

is as yet
immersed in the
pleasures of
youth; and I
advise that you
destroy the
Lutherans, and
Lady Truth, in
particular.

And gydit be Dame Sensualitie,

Rycht sa with ȝoung counsall intoxicate ;

1116 Swa at this tyme ȝe haif ȝour libertie.

To tak ȝour tyme, I hauld it best, for me,

And go distroy all thir Lutherians,

In speciall, ȝon ladie Veritie.

SPRITVALITIE.

Parson, contrive
this;

1120 Schir Persone, ȝe sall be my commissair,

To put this mater till executioun ;

and do you,

And ȝe, sir Freir, becaus ȝe can declair

Friar, assist.

The haill processe, pas with him in commissioun :

Bless you, both !

1124 Pas, all togidder, with my braid bennisoun ;

If free of speech,
imprison her,
not to approach
the King.

And, gif scho speiks against our libertie,

Then put hir in perpetuall presoun,

That scho cum nocht to King Humanitie.

(*Heir sall thay pas to Verity.*)

PERSONE.

What is your
business here ?

1128 Lustie Ladie, we wald faine vnderstand

Quhat earand ȝe haif in this Regioun.

Who authorized
your mission ?

To preich, or teich, quha gaif to ȝow command ?

To counsall Kingis how gat ȝe commissioun ?

Unless you
receive pardon,
and renounce
your errors, I
fear you will be
burnt alive.

1132 I dreid, without ȝe get ane remissioun,

And, syne, renunce ȝour new opiniones,

The sprituall stait sall put ȝow to perditioun,

And in the fyre will burne ȝow, flesche and bones.

VERITIE.

I recant nothing
I have spoken.

1136 I will recant nathing that I haue schawin :

I haue said nathing bot the veritie.

If the King gets
to know me, you
will rue my
coming.

Bot, with the King fra tyme that I be knawin,

I dreid ȝe spaiks of Spritualitie

1140 Sall rew that ever I came in this cuntrie :

Let him learn the
truth, and your
credit is at an
end

For, gif the Veritie plainlie war proclamit,

And, speciallie, to the Kings Maiestie,

For ȝour traditions ȝe wilbe all defamit.

FLATTRIE.

1144   Quhat buik is that, harlot, into thy hand ?   This is the New
       Out ! walloway ! this is the New Test'ment,   Testament, in
       In Englisch toung, and printit in England !   English, and
                                                       printed !
       Herisie ! herisie ! fire ! fire ! incontinent.   Heresy ! Fire !

VERITY.

1148   Forsuith, my freind, ȝe haue ane wrang   There is no
          iudgement ;   heresy in this
       For in this Buik thair is na heresie,   book, but Christ's
       Bot our Christs word, baith dulce and redolent,—   Word, a flowing
       Ane springing well of sinceir veritie.   well of truth.

DISSAIT.

1152   Cum on ȝour way : for all ȝour ȝealow locks,   You shall repent
       ȝour vantoun words, but doubt, ȝe sall repent :   your speeches in
                                                          the stocks to-
       This nicht ȝe sall forfair ane pair of stocks,   night, and be
       And, syne, the morne, be brocht to thoill Iudg-   tried to-morrow.
          ment.

VERITIE.

1156   For our Christs saik I am richt weill content   I am ready to
       To suffer all thing that sall pleis his grace.   suffer for Christ.
       Howbeit ȝe put ane thousand to torment,   Persecution
       Ten hundreth thowsand sall rise into thair place.   spreads faith.

       (*Veritie sits doun on hir knies, and sayis :*)

1160   Get vp !—thow sleipis all too lang, O Lord,—   Arise, O Lord !
       And mak sum ressonabill reformatioun   Convert those
                                                that trample on
       On them that dois tramp doun thy gracious word,   Thy Word and
       And hes ane deidlie indignatioun   set themselves
                                            against true
1164   At them quha maks maist trew narratioun.   teaching.
       Suffer me not, Lord, mair to be molest !   Let me not be
       Gude Lord, I mak the supplicatioun,   grieved and
                                               crushed by Thy
       With thy vnfreinds let me nocht be supprest.   enemies.
1168   Now, Lords, do as ȝe list.   Do your will,
                                         Lords.
           I haue na mair to say.   I have spoken.

FLATTRIE.

Rest here till
day.

Sit doun, and tak ȝow rest,
All nicht, till it be day.

Truth is put in
the stocks.

(*Thay put Veritie in the stocks, and returne to Spritualite.*)

DISSAIT.

We have made
fast the babbler.

1172   My Lord, wee haue, with diligence,
       Bucklit vp weill ȝon bledrand baird.

SPRITVALITIE.

You deserve
these ten crowns
as reward.

I think ȝe serue gude recompence.
Tak thir ten crowns for ȝour rewaird.

VERITY.

In me is fulfilled,
this day, the
prophecy, that
the truth must
suffer violence;
to be read in
Isaiah, chapter
lv.

1176   The Prophesie of the Propheit Esay
       Is practickit, alace ! on mee, this day,
       Quha said : the veritie sould be trampit doun
       Amid the streit, and put in strang presoun.
1180   His fyue and fiftie chapter quha list luik,
       Sall find thir words writtin in his Buik.

See, too, what S.
Paul says to
Timothy.

Richt sa, Sanct Paull wrytis to Timothie,
That men sall turne thair earis from veritie.

But I trust in
God to deliver
me.

1184   Bot in my Lord God I haue esperance :
       He will provide for my deliverance.

I fear, however,
that the
Spiritual Princes
will be visited by
the plagues of the
Apocalypse.

       Bot ȝe, Princes of Spritvalitie,
       Quha sould defend the sinceir veritie,
1188   I dreid the plagues of Iohnes Revelatioun
       Sall fal vpon thair generatioun.

Amend, and so

escape.

       I counsall ȝow this misse t'amend,
       Sa that ȝe may eschaip that fatall end.

CHASTITIE.

I have long been
banished.

I am unheeded
and unfriended.

1192   How lang sall this inconstant warld indure,
       That I sould baneist be sa lang, alace !
       Few creatures or nane takis on me cure,
       Quhilk gars me monie nicht ly harbrieles.

1196 Thocht I haue past all ȝeir, fra place to place,
      Amang the Temporal and Spirituall staits,
      Nor amang Princes, I can get na grace,
      Bot boustuouslie am halden at the ȝetis.

I wander from place to place, and neither the Temporal Estate, nor the Spiritual, nor Princes show me favour.

DILIGENCE.

1200 Ladie, I pray ȝow schaw me ȝour name.
      It dois me noy, ȝour lamentatioun.

What is your name? Your lament touches me.

CHASTITIE.

My freind, thairof I neid not to think shame ;
Dame Chastitie, baneist from town to town.

My name—of which I am not ashamed,—is Chastity.

DILIGENCE.

1204 Then pas to ladies of Religioun,
      Quhilk maks thair vow to obserue Chastitie.
      Lo ! quhair thair sits ane Priores of renown
      Amangs the rest of Spritualitie.

Go and try the nuns, especially a famous prioress.

CHASTITIE.

1208 I grant, ȝon Ladie hes vowit Chastitie
      For hir professioun ; thairto sould accord.
      Scho maid that vow for ane Abesie,
      Bot nocht for Christ Iesus our Lord.

She should be as good as her profession. Only she took not her vows for Christ.

1212 Fra tyme that thay get thair vows, I stand for'd,
      Thay banische hir out of thair cumpanie :
      With Chastitie thay can mak na concord,
      Bot leids thair lyfis in Sensualitie.

The nuns have banished Chastity, according better with Sensuality.

1216 I sall obserue ȝour counsall, gif I may.
      Cum on, and heir quhat ȝon Ladie will say.

Still, I will act on your advice.

(Chastitie passis to the Ladie Priores, and sayis :)

My prudent, lustie, Lastie Priores,
Remember how ȝe did vow Chastitie.

1220 Madame, I pray ȝow, of ȝour gentilnes,
      That ȝe wald pleis to haif of me pitie,
      And this ane nicht to gif me harberie :

As you have bound yourself to chastity, take pity on me, Madam, and give me shelter for this single night,

51

I pray you.
For this I mak ʒow supplicatioun.

Otherwise, so 1224 Do ʒe nocht sa, Madame, I dreid, perdie!

much the worse. It will be caus of depravatioun.

PRIORES.

Off at once! Pas hynd, Madame: be Christ! ʒe cum nocht heir:

You don't suit. ʒe are contrair to my cumplexioun.

Some old monk 1228 Gang seik ludging at sum auld Monk or Freir :
or friar may take
you in. Perchance thay will be ʒour protectioun.

Or apply to the Or to Prelats mak ʒour progressioun,

prelates. Quhilks ar obleist to ʒow, als weill as I.

Lady Sensuality 1232 Dame Sensuall hes geuin directioun
says I am not to
consort with you. ʒow till exclude out of my cumpany.

CHASTITIE.

If you wish to
learn more of the.
truth, the
Spiritual Lords,
too, have
excluded me
from their
presence. Gif ye wald wit mair of the veritie,

I sall schaw ʒow, be sure experience,

1236 How that the Lords of Sprituality

Hes baneist me, alace ! fra thair presence.

(Chastitie passes to the Lords of Spritualitie.)

My Lords, hail to My Lords, laud, gloir, triumph, and reverence

you! Mot be vnto ʒour halie Sprituall stait !

Of your
benevolence,
harbour me. 1240 I ʒow beseik, of ʒour benevolence,

To harbry mee that am sa desolait.

Far-travelled, I
can get no
lodging. Lords, I haue past throw mony vncouth schyre ;

Bot in this Land I can get na ludgeing.

As to my name, 1244 Of my name gif ʒe wald haif knawledging,

it is Chastity. Forsuith, my Lords, thay call me Chastitie.

Take me in to- I ʒow beseik, of ʒour graces bening,

night, for charity. Gif me ludging, this nicht, for charitie.

SPRITVALITIE.

Pass on, 1248 Pas on, Madame,—we knaw ʒow nocht ;—
stranger. -
Your staying here
any longer will
be paid dear for. Or, be him that the warld wrocht !

ʒour cumming sall be richt deir coft,

Gif ʒe mak langer tarie.

ABBOT.

1252 But doubt, wee will baith leif and die
    With our luif, Sensualitie.
    Wee will haif na mair deall with the
      Then with the Queene of Farie.

We prefer Sensuality, and will have no dealings with you.

PERSONE.

1256 Pas hame amang the Nunnis, and dwell,
    Quhilks ar of Chastitie the well.
    I traist thay will, with Buik and bell,
      Ressaue ȝow in thair Closter.

Go and stay with the nuns. They will give you a reception.

CHASTITIE.

1260 Sir, quhen I was the Nunnis amang,
    Out of thair dortour thay mee dang,
    And wald nocht let me bide sa lang
      To say my Pater noster :

The nuns drove me from their dormitory, before I could say a Pater Noster.

1264 I se na grace, thairfoir, to get.
    I hauld it best, or it be lait,
    For till go proue the Temporall stait,
      Gif thay will mee resaif.

I had better try, then, whether the Temporal Estate will take me in.

1268 Gud day, my Lord Temporalitie,
    And ȝow, merchant of gravitie !
    Ful faine wald I haue harberie,
      To ludge amang the laif.

My Lord Temporality, I would fain lodge with you.

TEMPORALITIE.

1272 Forsuith, wee wald be weil content
    To harbrie ȝow with gude intent,
    War nocht we haif impediment ;
      For quhy we twa ar maryit.

Gladly, but for the hindrance that we are married.

1276 Bot, wist our wyfis that ȝe war heir,
    Thay wald mak all this town on steir.
    Thairfoir, we reid ȝow rin areir,
      In dreid ȝe be miscaryit.

Considering our wives, you had better take yourself out of harm's reach.

4

CHASTITIE.

Ye men of craft,

house and feed

me, for Christ's

passion.

1280   3e men of craft, of greit ingyne,
         Gif me harbrie, for Christis pyne,
         And win Gods bennesone and myne,
             And help my hungrie hart.

SOWTAR.

You are welcome; 1284   Welcum, be him that maid the Mone!

and we will do   Till dwell with vs till it be Iune.

for you the bèst   We sall mend baith 3our hois and schone,

in our way.   And plainlie tak 3our part.

TAYLOVR.

Is this Lady   1288   Is this fair Ladie Chastitie?

Chastity? You   Now, welcum, be the Trinitie!

must not stay   I think it war ane great pitie

out there.   That thou sould ly thair out.

You have my   1292   3our great displeasour I forthink.

pity; and I   Sit doun, Madame, and tak ane drink;

propose that we   And let na sorrow in 3ow sink,

carouse together.   Bot let vs play cap'out.

SOWTAR.

I will join you.   1296   Fill in, and play cap'out;

                          For I am wonder dry.

And never   The Deuill snyp aff thair snout,

mind others.   That haits this company.

IENNIE.

Mother!   1300   Hoaw! mynnie, mynnie, mynnie!

TAYLOVRS WYFE.

Where is your   Quhat wald thow, my deir dochter Iennie?

father?   Iennie, my Ioy, quhair is thy dadie?

IENNY.

Drinking,   Mary! drinkand with ane lustie Ladie,

1304   Ane fair ʒoung mayden, cled in quhyte,
       Of quhom my dadie taks delyte.
       Scho hes the fairest forme of face,
       Furnischit with all kynd of grace.
1308   I traist, gif I can reckon richt,
       Scho schaips to ludge with him all nicht.

and happy, with a young maiden, a rare beauty who, I rather think, means to stay all night.

SOWTARS WYFE.

       Quhat dois the Sowtar, my gudman ?   ∨

What is the cobbler doing ?

JENNIE.

       Mary ! fillis the cap and turnes the can.
1312   Or he cum hame, be God ! I trow
       He will be drunkin lyke ane sow.

Toping; and he will be as drunk as a swine, before he comes home.

TAYLOVRS WYFE.

       This is ane greit dispyte, I think,
       For to resaue sic ane kow-clink.
1316   Quhat is ʒour counsell that wee do ?

What a shame to take in a harlot ! What shall we do

SOWTARS WYFE.

       Cummer, this is my counsall, lo !
       Ding ʒe the tane, and I the vther.

Let us give them a beating.

TAYLOVRS WYFE.

       I am content, be Gods mother !
1320   I think, for mee, thay huirsone smaiks
       Thay serue richt weill to get thair paiks.
       Quhat, maister feind, neids all this haist ?
       For it is half ane ʒeir, almaist,
1324   Sen ever that loun laborde my ledder.

So be it. This is what they deserve. It is six months since that scamp did me justice.

SOWTERS WYFE.

       God ! nor my trewker mence ane ledder !
       For it is mair nor fourtie dayis
       Sen ever he cleikit vp my clayis ;
1328   And, last quhen I gat chalmer glew,
       That foull Sowter began till spew.

And it is more than forty days since the cobbler showed me due benevolence ; and then he was sick over it.

And now thay will sit doun and drink
In company with ane kow-clink.
1332 Gif thay haif done vs this dispyte,
Let vs go ding them till thay dryte.

If they are really drinking with a harlot, let us give them a good dressing.

(*Heir the wifis sall chase away Chastitie.*)

TAYLOVRS WYFE.

Go hence, harlot! how durst thow be sa bauld
To ludge with our gudemen, but our licence?
1336 I mak ane vow to him that Iudas sauld,
This rock of myne sall be thy recompence.
Schaw me thy name, dudron, with diligence.

Here without our leave? You shall feel my distaff. What is your name?

CHASTITIE.

Marie! Chastitie is my name, be Sanct Blais!

Chastity.

TAYLOVRS WYFE.

1340 I pray God, nor he work on the vengence;
For I luifit, never, Chastitie, all my dayes.

That is what I never loved.

SOWTARS WYFE.

Bot my gudeman—the treuth I sall the tell,—
Gars mee keip Chastitie, sair agains my will.
1344 Becaus that Monstour hes maid sic ane mint,
With my bedstaf, that dastard beirs ane dint.
And, als, I vow, cum thow this gait againe,
Thy buttoks salbe beltit, be Sanct Blaine!

My husband makes me keep chaste. I am not to be trifled with; and I may show my spirit again.

(*Heir sall thay speik to thair gudemen, and ding them.*)

TAYLOVRS WYFE.

1348 Fals hurson carle, but dout thou sall forthink
That evar thow eat or drink with ȝon kow-clink.

You shall repent what you have done.

SOWTARS WYFE.

I mak ane vow to Sanct Crispine,
Ise be revengit on that graceles grume:
1352 And, to begin the play, tak, thair, ane flap.

As an earnest of my revenge, there is a blow.

SOWTAR.

The feind ressaue the hands that gaif mee that! Damn you!

SOWTARS WYFE.

Quhat now, huirsun? begins thow for til ban? Do you curse?
Tak, thair, ane vther vpon thy peild harne-pan. Take another
blow.
1356 Quhat, now, cummer? will thow nocht tak my Will you help
part? me, gossip?

TAYLOVRS WYFE.

That sal I do, cummer, with all my hart. Heartily.

(*Heir sall thay ding thair gudemen with silence.*)

TAYLOVR.

Alace! gossop, alace! how stands with ȝow? √ She has broken
ȝon cankart carling, alace! hes brokin my brow. my head.
1360 Now weils ȝow Preists, now weils ȝow, all ȝour Well is it with
lifes, the priests, not to
have such
That ar nocht weddit with sic wickit wyfes. wicked wives.

SOWTAR.

Bischops ar blist, howbeit that thay be waryit, And blessed
For thay may fuck thair fill, and be vnmaryit. are bishops.
1364 Gossop, alace! that blak band we may wary, Alas, that we
That ordanit sic puir men as vs to mary. must marry!
Quhat may be done bot tak in patience? Malediction
And on all wyfis we'ill cry ane loud vengence. on wives!

(*Heir sall the wyfis stand be the watter syde, and say :*)

SOWTARS WYFE.

1368 Sen of our cairls we have the victorie, Come off best,
what shall
Quhat is ȝour counsell, cummer, that be done? we do?

TAYLOVRS WYFE.

Send for gude wine, & hald our selfis merie : Send for wine,
I hauld this, ay, best, cummer, be Sanct Clone! and be merry.

SOWTARS WYFE.

I will go fill 1372 Cumer, will ȝe draw aff my hois & schone,
the quart.   To fill the Quart I sall rin to the toun.

TAYLOVRS WYFE.

Truss up your   That sal I do, be him that maid the Mone,
                   With all my hart : thairfoir, cummer, sit doun.
clothes, and make 1376 Kilt vp ȝour claithis abone ȝour waist, ·
haste back.   And speid ȝow hame againe in haist ;
I will get a   And I sall provyde for ane paist,
meal ready.   Our corsses to comfort.

SOWTARS WYFE.

I am afraid of the 1380 Then help me for to kilt my clais.
frogs, and of   Quhat gif the padoks nip my tais ?
drowning,   I dreid to droun heir, be Sanct Blais,
unless some one
supports me.   Without I get support.

(*Sho lifts vp hir clais aboue hir waist, & enters in the water.*)

But I shall not 1384 Cummer, I will nocht droun my sell,
drown, if I go
another way.   Go east about the nether mill.   ·

TAYLOVRS WYFE.

I will go with   I am content, be Bryds bell !
you by any road.   To gang with ȝow, quhair ever ȝe will.
                   (*Heir sall thay depairt, and pas to the Palȝeoun.*)

DILIGENCE TO CHASTITIE.

Why out so late? 1388 Madame, quhat gars ȝow gang sa lait ?
Which was   Tell me how ȝe haue done debait
kinder to you, the With the Temporall and Spirituall stait.
Temporal Estate,
or the Spiritual ?   Quha did ȝow maist kyndnes ?

CHASTITIE.

They both 1392 In faith, I fand bot ill, and war.
treated me like a   Thay gart mee stand fra thame askar,
beggar, and drove   Evin lyk ane begger at the bar,
me away,   And fleimit mair and lesse.

DILIGENCE.

1396   I counsall ȝow, but tarying,   <small>Go tell King</small>
         Gang tell Humanitie, the King.   <small>Humanity.</small>
         Perchance hee, of his grace bening,   <small>Perhaps he</small>
         Will mak to ȝow support.   <small>will aid you.</small>

CHASTITIE.

1400   Of ȝour counsell, I am content   <small>I accept your</small>
         To pas to him incontinent,   ·   <small>advice, hoping</small>
         And my service till him present,   <small>that good may</small>
         In hope of sum comfort.   <small>come of it.</small>
         (Heir sall thay pas to the King.)

DILIGENCE.

1404   Hoaw! Solace, gentil Solace, declair vnto the   <small>Solace, carry</small>
            king   <small>word to the King</small>
         How thair is heir ane Ladie, fair of face,   <small>that there is a</small>
         That in this cuntrie can get na ludging,   <small>fair lady here,</small>
         Bot pitifullie flemit from place to place,   <small>praying to be</small>
           <small>received at his</small>
1408   Without the king, of his speciall grace,   <small>Court, as a</small>
         As ane servand hir in his court resaif.   <small>servant.</small>
         Brother Solace, tell the king all the cace,   <small>Tell the news</small>
         That scho may be resavit amang the laif.   <small>persuasively.</small>

SOLACE.

1412   Soverane, get vp, and se ane hevinlie sicht,—   <small>Sire, look at this</small>
         Ane fair Ladie, in quhyt abuilȝement.   <small>fine creature,—</small>
         Scho may be peir vnto ane king, or knicht,—   <small>very like an</small>
         Most lyk ane Angell, be my iudgment.   <small>angel, methinks.</small>

REX HVMANITAS.

1416   I sall gang se that sicht, incontinent.   <small>I am coming.</small>
         Madame, behauld gif ȝe haue knawledging   <small>See whether you</small>
           <small>know her, or</small>
         Of ȝon Ladie, or quhat is hir intent.   <small>her business.</small>
           <small>I shall not</small>
         Thairefter wee sall turne, but tarying.   <small>neglect her.</small>

SENSVALITIE.

It may be that
I know her.
It is Chastity.
As she and I
cannot stay in
one place, if you
prefer my
company, Sire,
send her, at once,
out of the
country.

1420 Sir, let me se quhat 30n mater may meine :
Perchance that I may knaw hir be hir face.
But doubt, this is Dame Chastitie, I weine.
Sir, I and scho cannot byde in ane place ;
1424 But, gif it be the pleasour of 30ur grace
That I remaine into 30ur company,
This woman richt haistelie gar chase,
That scho na mair be sene in this cuntry.

REX HVMANITAS.

Be it just as you
please. I submit
the matter to
your decision.

1428 As ever 3e pleis, sweit hart, sa sall it be.
Dispone hir as 3e think expedient,
Evin as 3e list, to let hir liue or die.
I will refer that thing to 30ur Iudgement.

SENSVALITIE.

Then let her be
expelled the
country, to die,
if she returns.
Sapience and
Discretion, do
your duty.

1432 I will that scho be flemit incontinent,
And never to cum againe in this cuntrie ;
And, gif scho dois, but doubt scho sall repent,
As, als, perchance, a duilfull deid sall die.
1436 Pas on, sir Sapience, and Discretioun,
And banische hir out of the kings presence.

DISCRETIOVN.

Madam, we
obey you,
obligingly.
Lady Chastity,
come and be set
in the stocks.

That sall we do, Madame, be Gods passioun !
Wee sall do 30ur command with diligence,
1440 And at 30ur hand serue gudely recompence.
Dame Chastitie, cum on : be not agast :
Wee sall, rycht sone, vpon 30ur awin expence,
Into the stocks 30ur bony fute mak fast.

(*Heir sall they harl Chastitie to the stocks ; and scho sall say :*

Patience, sirs.
I yield to your
commands,

1444 I pray 30w, sirs, be patient ;
For I sall be obedient
Till do quhat 3e command,

Sen I se thair is na remeid,

having no choice

1448 Howbeit it war to suffer deid,

but death or

Or flemit furth of the land.

banishment.

I wyte the Empreour Constantine,

The Emperor

That I am put to sic ruine,

Constantine is to

1452 And baneist from the Kirk ;

blame for my

For, sen he maid the Paip ane King,

disfavour,—the

In Rome I could get na ludging ;

fruit of his

Bot heidlangs in the mirk.

having made the

1456 Bot Ladie Sensualitie

Pope a king.

Lady Sensuality,

Sen syne hes gydit this cuntrie,

since then, has

And monie of the rest ;

And now scho reulis all this land,

borne sway, and

1460 And hes decryit, at hir command,

has ordered that

That I suld be supprest.

I be put down.

Bot all comes for the best

But good comes

Til him that louis the Lord :

to the good; and

1464 Thocht I be now molest,

I hope for better

I traist to be restorde.

fortune.

(Heir sall they put hir in the stocks.)

Sister, alace ! this is ane cairful cace,

It is sad that we should be so

That we with Princes sould be sa abhorde :

abhorred by kings.

VERITY.

1468 Be blyth, sister. I trust, within schort space,

We shall soon be

That we sall be richt honorablie restorde,

well with

And with the King we sall be at concorde ;

the king;

For I heir tell, divyne Correctioun

for Correction has

1472 Is new landit, thankit be Christ our Lord !

arrived, and will

I wait hee will be our protectioun.

protect us.

(Hir sall enter Corrections Varlet.)

VARLET.

Sirs, stand abak, and hauld ȝow coy.

I am Correction's servant, come to

I am the King Correctiouns boy,

prepare a place

1476 Cum heir to dres his place.

for him.

Yield		Se that 3e mak obedience
obedience		Vntill his nobill excellence,
to him, at sight.		Fra tyme 3e se his face ;
He is reforming	1480	For he maks reformatiouns
the nations of		Out-throw all Christin Natiouns,
Christendom,		Quhair he finds great debaits :
and will do		And, sa far as I vnderstand,
here as	1484	He sall reforme, into this Land,
elsewhere.		Evin all the thrie estaits.
God has sent him,		God furth of heavin hes him send,
to punish		To punische all that dois offend
offenders	1488	Against his Maiestie ;
with wars,		As lyks him best, to tak vengence,
plagues, death,		Sumtyme with Sword and Pestilence,
and poverty.		With derth and povertie.
To the penitent	1492	Bot, quhen the peopill dois repent,
he will show		And beis to God obedient,
grace;		Then will he gif them grace :
but the		Bot thay that will nocht be correctit
obstinate he	1496	Rycht sudanlie will be deiectit,
will cast down.		And fleimit from his face.
Our words are		Sirs, thocht wee speik in generall,
intended		Let na man into speciall
for all ;	1500	Tak our words at the warst.
and you must		Quhat ever wee do, quhat ever wee say,
take them in		I pray 3ow tak it all in play,
good part.		And iudg, ay, to the best.
I will make haste	1504	For silence I protest
now, and give		Baith of Lord, Laird, and Ladie.
notice that all is		Now I will rin, but rest,
made ready.		And tell that all is ready.

DISSAIT.

This news of	1508	Brother, heir 3e 3on proclamatioun ?
reformation		I dreid full sair of reformatioun :
stuns me.		3on message maks me mangit.

62

Quhat is ȝour counsell, to me tell.
1512 Remaine wee heir, be God him sell!
Wee will be, all thre, hangit.

What do you advise? For, if we stay here, we shall be hanged.

FLATTRIE.

Ile gang to Spiritualitie,
And preich out-throw his dyosie,
1516   Quhair I will be vnknawin;
Or keip me closse into sum closter,
With mony piteous Pater noster,
    Till all thir blasts be blawin.

I will go and preach where I am unknown, or will keep close, in some cloister, till more quiet times.

DISSAIT.

1520 Ile be weill treitit, as ȝe ken,
With my maisters, the merchand men,
    Quhilk can mak small debait.
Ȝe ken richt few of them that thryfes,
1524 Or can begyll the landwart wyfes,
    But me, thair man, Dissait.
Now, Falset, quhat sall be thy schift?

My masters, the merchants, will look after me; for few of them can thrive without Deceit. And you, Falsehood?

FALSET.

Na, cuir thow nocht, man, for my thrift.
1528   Trows thou that I be daft?
Na, I will leif ane lustie lyfe
Withoutin ony sturt and stryfe,
    Amang the men of craft.

I for myself. Am I mad? I shall do bravely among the craftsmen.

FLATTRIE.

1532 I na mair will remaine besyd ȝow,
Bot counsell ȝow, rycht weill to gyde ȝow,
    Byd nocht on Correctioun.
Fair-weil! I will na langer tarie.
1536 I pray the alrich Queene of Farie
    To be ȝour protectioun.

My counsel is, not to stay for Correction. Good bye! May the Queen of the Fays defend you!

DISSAIT.

Falset, I wald wee maid ane band.

Let us conspire,

63

1540

Now, quhill the King is ʒit sleipand,
Quhat rack to steill his Box ?

FALSET.

Now, weill said, be the Sacrament !
I sall it steill incontinent,
Thocht it had twentie lox.

(Heir sall Falset steill the Kings box with silence.)

1544

Lo ! heir the Box : now let vs ga :
This may suffice for our rewairds.

DISSAIT.

1548

ʒea, that it may, man, be this day :
It may weill mak of landwart lairds.
Now let vs cast away our clais,
In dreid sum follow on the chase.

FALSET.

Rycht weill deuysit, man, be Sanct Blais !
Wald God wee war out of this place !

DISSAIT.

1552

Now, sen thair is na man to wrang vs,
I pray ʒow, brother, with my hart,
Let vs ga part this pelf amang vs ;
Syne, haistely we sall depart.

FALSET.

1556

Trows thou to get als mekill as I ?
That sall thow nocht : I staw the Box.
Thou did nathing bot luikit by,
Ay lurkeand lyke ane wylie Fox.

DISSAIT.

1560

Thy heid sall beir ane cuppill of knox,
Pellour, without I get my part.
Swyith ! huirsun smaik, ryfe vp the lox,

Or I sall stick the throuch the hart.

(*Heir sall thay fecht with silence.*)

FALSET.

1564 Alace! for ever my eye is out.
Walloway! will na man red the men?

DISSAIT.

Vpon thy craig tak thair ane clout.
To be courtesse I sall the ken.
1568 Fair-weill! for I am at the flicht :
I will nocht byde on ma demands.
And wee twa meit againe this nicht,
Thy feit salbe with fourtie hands.

(*Heir sal Dissait rin away with the Box, throuch the water.*)

DIVYNE CORRECTIOVN.

1572 Beati qui esuriunt & sitiunt Iustitiam.
Thir ar the words of the redoutit Roy,
The Prince of peace, aboue all Kings King,
Quhilk hes me sent all cuntries to convoye,
1576 And all misdoars dourlie to doun thring.
I will do nocht without the conveining
Ane Parleament of the estaits all :
In thair presence I sall, but feinȝeing,
1580 Iniquitie vnder my Sword doun thrall.
Thair may no Prince do acts honorabill,
Bot gif his counsall thairto will assist.
How may he knaw the thing maist profitabil,
1584 To follow vertew, and vycis to resist,
Without he be instructit and solist?
And, quhen the King stands at his counsell sound,
Then welth sall wax, and plentie, as he list ;
1588 And policie sall in his Realme abound.
Gif ony list my name for till inquyre,
I am callit Divine Correctioun.

Marginal glosses:

or I stab you.

My eye is out.
Will no one
separate them?

There is a clout
for your civility.
I am going, with
what I have;
and you will not
see me
again soon.

Blessed are they
who rightly
consider justice.
So says He who
has sent me to
repress
transgressors.
Supported by the
three Estates, I
purpose to put an
end to iniquity.
Like council,
like king.
A king, to do
aright, requires
guidance.
If he is heedful,
great is the
reward.
My name is
Correction.

I profit all
nations;

1592

I fled throch mony vncouth land & schyre,
To the greit profit of ilk Natioun.

and I have come

Now am I cum into this Regioun,

here to right all

To teill the ground that hes bene lang vnsaw

manner of

To punische tyrants for thair transgressioun,

wrongs.

1596

And to caus leill men liue vpon thair awin.

I am all

Na Realme nor Land but my support may sta

to kings.

For I gar Kings liue into Royaltie.

Rich and poor

To rich and puir I beir ane equall hand,

are alike to me.

1600

That thay may liue into thair awin degrie :

I bring
tranquillity ; and
I put down and
punish traitors
and tyrants.

1604

Quhair I am nocht is no tranquillitie.
Be me tratours and tyrants ar put doun,—
Quha thinks na schame of thair iniquitie,
Till thay be punisched be mee, Correctioun.

What is a king
but an officer
busied in securing
equity and in
admonishing
trespassers ?

1608

Quhat is ane King ? nocht bot ane officiar
To caus his Leiges liue in equitie,
And, vnder God, to be ane punischer
Of trespassours against his Maiestie.

If the king is a
tyrant, then
follow war,
poverty, and
shameful
slaughter.

1612

Bot, quhen the King dois liue in tyrannie,
Breakand Iustice, for feare, or affectioun,
Then is his Realme in weir and povertie,
With schamefull slauchter, but correctioun.

I am a judge,

I am ane Iudge richt potent and seveir,

come from afar,

Cum, to do Iustice, monie thowsand myle :

unwavering,

I am sa constant, baith in peice and weir,

unseducible.

1616

Na bud nor fauour may my sicht oversyle.

Many grieve at
my advent;

Thair is, thairfoir, richt monie, in this Ile,
Of my repair, but doubt, that dois repent.

but the virtuous

Bot verteous men, I traist, sall on me smyle,

rejoice thereat.

1620

And of my cumming sall be richt weill conten

GVDE COVNSELL.

The faithful

Welcum, my Lord, welcum, ten thousand tym

welcome you,

Till all faithfull men of this Regioun !

come to correct

Welcum, for till correct all falts and cryms

faults and crimes.

1624

Amang this cankerd congregatioun !

Louse Chastitie, I mak supplicatioun :   *Release Chastity*
Put till fredome fair Ladie Veritie,   *and Lady Truth,*
Quha be vnfaithfull folk of this Natioun   *now lying in*
1628   Lyis bund full fast into Captivitie.   *captivity.*

CORRECTIOVN.

I mervel, Gude-counsell, how that may be.   *`Are not you*
Ar ȝe nocht with the King familiar ?   *friends with the king ?*

GVDE COVNSELL.

That I am nocht, my Lord, full wa is me !   *On the*
1632   Bot, lyke ane begger, am halden at the bar :   *contrary,*
Thay play bo-keik, evin as I war ane skar.   *I am held aloof.*
Thair came thrie knaues, in cleithing counterfeit,   *Three knaves*
And fra the King thay gart me stand affar,—   *kept me from*
1636   Quhais names war Flattrie, Falset, and Dissait ;   *the king.*
Bot, quhen thay knaues hard tell of ȝour cum-   *Hearing of your*
    ming,   *coming, they*
Thay staw away, ilk ane, ane sindrie gait,   *stole off, each in a separate*
And cuist fra them thair counterfit cleithing.   *direction,*
1640   For thair leuing full weill thay can debait.   *self-helpful ;*
The merchandmen thay haif resauit Dissait ;   *Deceit to the*
As for Falset, my Lord, full weill I ken,   *merchants,*
He will be richt weill treitit, air and lait,   *Falsehood to the*
1644   Amang the maist part of the crafts men ;   *craftsmen,*
Flattrie hes taine the habite of ane Freir,   *and Flattery to*
Thinkand to begyll Spiritualitie.   *the Spirituality.*

CORRECTIOVN.

But dout, my freind and I liue half ane ȝeir,   *We shall find out*
1648   I sall search out that great iniquitie.   *all shortly.*
Quhair lyis ȝon Ladyes in Captiuitie ?   *Where are the ladies ?*
How, now, Sisters ? quha hes ȝow sa disgysit ?   *How disguised !*

VERITIE.

Vnfaithfull members of iniquitie,   *The wicked have*
1652   Dispytfullie, my Lord, hes vs supprysit.   *oppressed us.*

CORRECTIOVN.

Release the
ladies, and break
the stocks.
Gang put ʒon Ladyis to thair libertie,

Incontinent, and break doun all the stocks.

And be in good
But doubt, thay ar full deir welcum to mee.

earnest.   1656   Mak diligence : me think ʒe do bot mocks.

Break the locks,
Speid hand, and spair nocht for to break the

and take them by
  locks ;

the hand.
And tenderlie tak them vp be the hand.

I would fain
Had I them heir, thay knaues suld ken my

assault their
  knocks,

persecutors.   1660   That them opprest, and baneist aff the land.

  (*Thay tak the Ladyis furth of the stocks ; and Veritie sall say :*)

VERITIE.

And now, Sire, I
beg you to go to
King Humanity,
and to dismiss
from his service
Lady Sensuality,
in favour of Good
Counsel.
Wee thank ʒou, sir, of ʒour benignitie.

Bot I beseik ʒour maiestie Royall,

That ʒe wald pas to King Humanitie,

1664   And fleime from him ʒon Ladie Sensuall,

And enter in his service Gude-counsell ;

For ye will find him verie counsalabill.

CORRECTIOVN.

It shall be so;
and he will stand
by you three.
Cum on, Sisters : as ʒe haif said, I sall,

1668   And gar him stand with ʒow thrie, firme and

  stabill.

  (*Correctioun passis towards the King, with Veritie, Chastitie,
and Gude-counsell.*)

WANTONNES.

Who is it that I
see, ready to
flee away ?
What means
this ?
Is he friend,
or foe ?
What says he?
I know him not.
Solace, knawis thou not quhat I se ?

Ane knicht, or ellis ane king, thinks me,

With wantoun wings, as he wald fle.

  Brother, quhat may this meine ?

I vnderstand nocht, be this day,

Quhidder that he be freind or fay.

Stand still, and heare quhat he will say.

  Sic ane I haif nocht seine.

1672 (beside "What means this ?")
1676 (beside "I know him not.")

SOLACE.

Ʒon is ane stranger, I stand forde :

He semes to be ane lustie Lord.

Be his heir-cumming for concorde,

1680   And be kinde till our King,

He sall be welcome to this place,

And treatit with the Kingis grace :

Be it nocht sa, we sall him chace,

1684   ˙ And to the diuell him ding !

If this stranger proves to be well-disposed to the King, he shall be welcome and favoured. Otherwise, we will drive him off.

PLACEBO.

I reid vs put vpon the King,

And walkin him of his sleiping.

Sir, rise, and se ane vncouth thing !

1688   ˙ Get vp ! Ʒe ly too lang.

Let us wake the King. Up, Sire, and see a strange thing!

SENSVALITIE.

Put on ʒour hude, Iohne-Fule.   Ʒe raif.

How dar ʒe be so pert, sir knaif,

To tuich the King ?   Sa Christ me saif,

1692   Fals huirsone, thow sall hang.˙

How dare you touch the King? You shall be hanged.

CORRECTIOVN.

Get vp, sir King !   Ʒe haif sleipit aneuch

Into the armis of Ladie Sensual.

Be suir that mair belangis to the pleuch ;

1696   As efterward, perchance, rehears I sall.

Remember how the King Sardanapall

Amang fair Ladyes tuke his lust sa lang,

Sa that the maist pairt of his Leiges al

1700   Rebeld, and syne him duilfully doun thrang.

Remember how, into the tyme of Noy,

For the foull stinck and sin of lechery,

God, be my wande, did al the warld destroy.

1704   Sodome and Gomore, richt sa, full rigorously,

For that vyld sin, war brunt maist cruelly.

Thairfoir, I the command, incontinent

You have had sleep enough. More misbecomes you. King Sardanapalus, lustful, was dethroned. Under Noah, for lechery the world was destroyed. Therefor, too, Sodom and Gomorrah were burnt. Accordingly,

5

banish Sensuality,
if you would
not repent. 1708

Banische from the that huir Sensualitie ;
Or els, but doubt, rudlie thow sall repent.

REX HVMANITAS.

Who authorized
you to correct
a King ?

I am King
Humanity, a
royal sovereign. 1712

Be quhom haue ȝe sa greit authoritie,
Quha dois presume for til correct ane King ?
Knaw ȝe nocht me, greit King Humanitie,
That in my Regioun Royally dois ring ?

CORRECTIOVN.

I have power to

ruin princes that,

unrepentantly,

live amiss. · 1716

First, I reform

you; then,

your subjects.

Out, harlot ! 1720

I haue power greit Princes to doun thring,
That liues contrair the Maiestie Divyne,
Against the treuth quhilk plainlie dois maling :
Repent they nocht, I put them to ruyne.
I will begin at thee, quhilk is the head,
And mak on the, first, reformatioun :
Thy Leiges, than, will follow the, but pleid.
Swyith ! harlot.   Hence, without dilatioun.

SENSVALITIE.

Let me return

to Rome.

Among its
princes I
shall thrive. 1724

Adieu ! It does

not matter.

My curse on you,

following my foes! 1728

Pitiful King! ·

Bishops and
Cardinals would
pamper me.
There is no
earthly joy 1732
without me.

My Lord, I mak ȝow supplicatioun,
Gif me licence to pas againe to Rome.
Amang the Princes of that Natioun,
I lat ȝow wit, my fresche beautie will blume.
Adeu, Sir King ! I may na langer tary.
I cair nocht that : als gude luife cums as gais.
I recommend ȝow to the Queene of Farie.
I se ȝe will be gydit with my fais.
As for this king, I cure him nocht twa strais.
War I amang Bischops and Cardinals,
I wald get gould, silver, and precious clais.
Na earthlie ioy, but my presence, avails.

(*Heir sall scho pas to Spiritualitie.*)

Venus preserve
you, Lord
Spiritual.

I cannot resist. .

My Lords of the Spirituall stait,
Venus preserue ȝow, air and lait ;
For I can mak na mair debait.

1736   I am partit with ȝour king,   *I have left your King, being banished by counsel of Correction.*
    And am baneischt this Regioun,
    Be counsell of Correctioun.
    Be ȝe nocht my protectioun,   *You are my*
1740   I may seik my ludgeing.   *sole resort.*

SPIRITVALITIE.

    Welcum, our dayis darling!   *Welcome, darling,*
    Welcum, with all our hart!   *heartily. We*
    Wee, all, but feinȝeing,   *will, all, be on*
1744   Sall plainly tak ȝour part.   *your side.*

(Heir sal the Bishops, Abbots, and Persons kis the Ladies.)

CORRECTIOVN.

    Sen ȝe ar quyte of Sensualitie,   *Quit of Sensuality,*
    Resaue into ȝour service Gude-counsall,   *entertain Good Counsel; also Chastity, till*
    And, richt sa, this fair Ladie Chastitie,
1748   Till ȝe mary sum Queene of blude-royall :   *you marry,*
    Observe, then, Chastitie matrimoniall.   *and after;*
    Richt sa, resaue Veritie be the hand.   *and Truth.*
    Vse thair counsell, ȝour fame sall never fall :   *Advise with them, and agree with them.*
1752   With thame, thairfoir, mak ane perpetuall band.

(Heir sall the King resaue Counsell, Veritie, & Chastitie.)

    Now, sir, tak tent quhat I will say ;   *Listen to them,*
    Observe thir same, baith nicht and day,   *Sire, night and*
    And let them never part ȝow fray ;   *day, at your side;*
1756   Or els, withoutin doubt,   *else, if you turn*
    Turne ȝe to Sensualitie,   *to Sensuality, you*
    To vicious lyfe, and rebaldrie,
    Out of ȝour Realme, richt schamefullie,   *will be expelled*
1760   Ȝe sall be ruttit out ;   *from your realm;*
    As was Tarquine, the Romane King   *as was Tarquin,*
    Quha was, for his vicious living,   *who, for*
    And for the schamefull ravisching   *ravishing chaste Lucretia, was*
1764   Of the fair chaist Lucres,   *deprived of*
    He was digraidit of his croun,   *his crown,*

And baneist aff his Regioun.
I maid on him correctioun,

1768   As stories dois expres.

REX HVMANITAS.

I am content to ȝour counsall t'inclyne,
ȝe beand of gude conditioun.
At ȝour command sall be all that is myne;
And heir I gif ȝow full commissioun
To punische faults and gif remissioun.
To all vertew I salbe consociabill:
With ȝow I sall confirme ane vnioun,
And at ȝour counsall stand, ay, firme and stabill.

I trust you,

worthy of trust.

Submissive, I
permit you to
punish and
to forgive.

I will make a
league with you,
and will abide by
your counsel.

1772

1776

(The King imbraces Correction, with a humbil countenance.)

CORRECTIOVN.

I counsall ȝow, incontinent
To gar proclame ane Parliament
    Of all the thrie estaits,
That thay be heir, with diligence,
To mak to ȝow obedience,
    And, syne, dres all debaits.

Convene, at once,

a Parliamont of

the three Estates;

and then address

yourself to

complaints.

1780

REX HVMANITAS.

That salbe done but mair demand.
Hoaw! Diligence, cum heir, fra hand,
    And tak ȝour informatioun.
Gang warne the Spiritualitie,
Rycht sa, the Temporalitie,
    Be oppin proclamatioun,
In gudlie haist for to compeir,
In thair maist honorabill maneir,
    To gif vs thair counsals.
Quha that beis absent, to them schaw,
That thay sall vnderly the law,
    And punischt be, that fails.

Even so.

Diligence, learn
your message.

Go warn the
Spirituality and
the Temporalty
to give their
speedy attend-
ance, to advise us.

Negligence to
comply will
be punished.

1784

1788

1792

DILIGENCE.

Sir, I sall, baith in bruch and land,
1796   With diligence do ȝour command,
    Vpon my awin expens.
Sir, I haue servit ȝow all this ȝeir ;
Bot I gat never ane dinneir,
1800   Ȝit, for my recompence.

I will serve you, and at my own charges. For all this year's services I have got no recompence.

REX HVMANITAS.

Pas on, and thou salbe regairdit,
And, for thy service, weill rewairdit ;
  For quhy, with my consent,
1804 Thou sall haue, ȝeirly, for thy hyre,
The teind mussellis of the ferrie myre,
  Confirmit in Parliament.

You shall be well rewarded; and the reward shall be confirmed in Parliament.

DILIGENCE.

I will get riches throw that rent,
1808   Efter the day of Dume ;
Quhen, in the colpots of Tranent,
    Butter will grow on brume.
All nicht I had sa meikill drouth,
1812   I micht nocht sleip ane wink.
Or I proclame ocht with my mouth,
    But doubt I man haif drink.

And no doubt I shall be very rich by it. All night I slept not for thirst. Before I cry, I must have a drink.

CORRECTIOVN.

Cum heir, Placebo and Solace,
1816 With ȝour companȝeoun, Wantonnes.
    I knaw weill ȝour conditioun :
For tysting King Humanitie
To resaue Sensualitie,
1820   Ȝe man suffer punitioun.

Placebo, Solace, and Wantonness, you, for enticing King Humanity to receive Sensuality, must be punished.

WANTONNES.

We grant, my lord, we haue done ill ;

We have done wrong ;

so we yield.

Yet, deceived,
we really thought
there was no
harm in lechery,
it being so
common.

Thairfoir, wee put vs in ȝour will.
Bot wee haife bene abusit ;
1824 For, in gude faith, Sir, wee beleifit
That lecherie had na man greifit,
Becaus it is sa vsit.

PLACEBO.

Sensuality is
countenanced,
everywhere, by
the great, and
even by our
own prelates.

Ask my Lady
Prioress if
lechery be sin.

ȝe se how Sensualitie
1828 With Principals of ilk cuntrie
Bene glaidlie lettin in,
And with our Prelatis, mair and les.
Speir at my Ladie Priores
1832 Gif lechery be sin.

SOLACE.

We will amend,

if pardoned.

But let us sing,

dance, &c., &c.,

for the King's

pleasure.

Sir, wee sall mend our conditioun,
Sa ȝe giue vs remissioun.
Bot giue vs liue to sing,
1836 To dance, to play at Chesse and Tabils,
To reid Stories and mirrie fabils,
For pleasure of our King.

CORRECTIOVN.

Take your
pardon,
conditionally.

Of course
Princes may
divert themselves
harmlessly, as
with hawking
and hunting,

in time

of peace,

and with
throwing the
spear, against
using it in war.

Sa that ȝe do na vther cryme,
1840 ȝe sall be pardonit at this tyme ;
For quhy, as I suppois,
Princes may sumtyme seik solace
With mirth and lawful mirrines,
1844 Thair spirits to reioyis.
And, richt sa, Halking and Hunting
Ar honest pastimes for ane King,
Into the tyme of peace ;
1848 And leirne to rin ane heavie spear,
That he, into the tyme of wear,
May follow at the cheace.

REX HVMANITAS.

Quhair is Sapience and Discretioun ?
1852 And quhy cums nocht Devotioun nar ?   ·

Where are
Sapience,
Discretion, and
Devotion ?

VERITIE.

Sapience, sir, was ane verie loun ;
And Discretioun was nathing war.
The suith, Sir, gif I wald report,
1856 Thay did begyle зour Excellence,
And wald not suffer to resort
Ane of vs thrie to зour presence.

Sapience and
Discretion were
sad fellows. To
say truth, they
deceived you, and
prevented our
getting access
to you.

CHASTITIE.

Thay thrie war Flattrie, and Dissait,
1860 And Falset,—that vnhappie loun,—
Against vs thrie quhilk maid debait,
And baneischt vs from town to town.
Thay gart vs twa fall into sowne,
1864 Quhen thay vs lockit in the stocks.
That dastart knaue, Discretioun,
Full thrifteouslie did steill зour Box.

They were,
really, Flattery,
Deceit, and
Falsehood ;
and they drove
us from town
to town,
and put us
in the stocks.

Discretion
stole your box.

REX HVMANITAS.

The Deuill tak them, sen thay ar gane !
1868 Me thocht them, ay, thrie verie smaiks.
I mak ane vow to Sanct Mavane,
Quhen I them finde, thays bear thair paiks :
I se they haue playit me the glaiks.
1872 Gude-counsall, now schaw me the best,
Quhen I fix on зow thrie my staiks,
How I sall keip my Realme in rest.
Initium sapientiæ est timor Domini.

The Devil take
the rascals !

If I find them,
they shall be
paid for
fooling me.

Good Counsel,
now show me
how, relying on
you three, I can
keep my realm
in quiet.

GVDE-COVNSALL.

1876 Sir, gif зour hienes зearnis lang to ring,
First, dread зour God, abuif all vther thing ;

If you would
reign long,
fear God ;

for you are but
an instrument
in His hands,
appointed to rule
His people.

For ʒe ar bot ane mortall instrument
To that great God and King Omnipotent,
1880 Preordinat, be his divine Maiestie,
To reull his peopill intill vnitie.

First, let a king
be just; next,
merciful, without
severity or
partiality.

The principall point, Sir, of ane kings office
Is for to do to euerilk man iustice,
1884 And for to mix his iustice with mercie,
But rigour, fauour, or parcialitie.

To govern is a
grave thing.

Forsuith, it is na littill obseruance,
Great Regions to haue in gouernance.

A king has his
choice between
great labour and
perpetual
infamy.

1888 Quha euer taks on him that kinglie cuir,
To get ane of thir twa, he suld be suir,—
Great paine and labour, and that continuall,
Or ellis to haue defame perpetuall.

Of some the
fame, of others
the shame, will
be rehearsed a
thousand years
after they
are dead,

1892 Quha guydis weill they win immortall fame ;
Quha the contrair, they get perpetuall schame ;
Efter quhais death, but dout, ane thousand ʒeir
Thair life at lenth rehearst sall be, perqueir.

Study the
chronicles; for
there you will
learn that the
deeds of a prince
never die.

1896 The Chroniklis to knaw I ʒow exhort :
Thair sall ʒe finde baith gude and euill report ;
For euerie Prince, efter his qualitie,
Thocht he be deid, his deids sall neuer die.

Obey me, and
be glorious.

1900 Sir, gif ʒe please for to vse my counsall,
ʒour fame and name sall be perpetuall.

*(Heir sall the messinger Diligence returne and cry a Hoyzes, a
Hoyzes, a Hoyzes, and say :)*

King Humanity
charges all
members of
Parliament to
repair to the
Court forthwith,
in due form.

At the command of King Humanitie,
I wairne and charge all members of Parliament,
1904 Baith sprituall stait and Temporalitie,
That till his Grace thay be obedient,
And speid them to the Court, incontinent,
In gude ordour arrayit royally.

Let none be
absent or
contumacious.

1908 Quha beis absent, or inobedient,
The Kings displeasure thay sall vnderly.

Also, as you have
heard the first
half of our play,

And, als, I mak ʒow exhortatioun,
Sen ʒe haif heard the first pairt of our play,

1912 Go tak ane drink, and mak Collatioun :   *refresh your-*
    Ilk man drink till his marrow, I ȝow pray.   *selves, and pledge*
    each other.

    Tarie nocht lang : it is lait in the day.   *Be quick.*

    Let sum drink Ayle, and sum drink Claret wine :   *Let some*

1916 Be great Doctors of Physick I heare say,   *drink ale;*
    others, claret,
    That michtie drink comforts the dull ingine.   *comforting.*

    And ȝe, Ladies, that list to pisch,   *Let the ladies,*

    Lift vp ȝour taill plat in ane disch ;   *too, avail them-*

1920 And, gif that ȝour mawkine cryis quhisch,   *selves of this*

    Stop in ane wusp of stray.   *intermission.*

    Let nocht ȝour bladder burst, I pray ȝow ;   *Do not be pre-*
    vented from
    For that war euin aneuch to slay ȝow :   *returning ; for*
    the best part
1924 For ȝit thair is to cum, I say ȝow,   *of the play is*

    The best pairt of our Play.   *still behind.*

    The End of the first part of the Satyre.

(Now sall the pepill mak Collatioun : then beginnis the Inter-
lude ; the Kings, Bischops, and principall players being out of
their seats.)

PAVPER, THE PVRE MAN.

O f ȝour almis, gude folks, for Gods luife of   *Give me alms,*
    heavin !   *good people, for*
    my motherless
    For I haue motherles bairns, either sax or seavin.   *little ones ; or,*

1928 Gif ȝe'ill gif me na gude, for the luife of Iesus,   *at least, direct me*

    Wische me the richt way till Sanct-Androes.   *to S. Andrews.*

DILIGENCE.

    Quhair haue wee gottin this gudly companȝeoun?   *Be off,*

    Swyith ! Out of the feild, fals raggit loun !   *wretch !*

1932 God wait gif heir be ane weill keipit place,   *How came*

    Quhen sic ane vilde begger Carle may get entres.   *he here ?*

How negligent, Fy on ȝow officiars, that mends nocht thir
 failȝies !

both provost I gif ȝow all till the deuill, baith Provost and

and bailies !   Bailȝies.

Off with this
clown; or no
more play. 1936 Without ȝe cum and chase this Carle away,
 The Deuill a word ȝe'is get mair of our play.

Why such Fals huirsun, raggit Carle, quhat Deuil is that

violence ?   thou rugs ?

PAVPER.

Shall I cut Quha Devil maid the ane gentill man, that wald

your ears off ?   not cut thy lugs ?

DILIGENCE.

Take yourself 1940 Quhat, now ! Me thinks the carle begins to crack.

away; or I will Swyith, carle ! Away ! Or be this day Ise break

break your back.   thy back.

(*Heir sall the Curle clim vp and sit in the Kings tchyre.*)

Come down; or I Cum doun ; or, be Gods croun ! fals loun, I sall

will murder you.   slay the.

PAVPER.

These dastardly Now, sweir be thy brunt schinis.   The Deuill

courtiers, as soon   ding them fra the !

as they get whole 1944 Quhat say ȝe till thir court dastards ?   Be thay

clothes, learn to   get hail clais,

swear and to Sa sune do thay leir to sweir, and trip on thair

trip daintily.   tais.

DILIGENCE.

He called me Me thocht the carle callit me knaue, evin in my

knave, to the face.   face.

Ask pardon; or Be Sanct Fillane ! thou salbe slane, bot gif thou

be slain.   ask grace.

Come down; or
you shall lose
your head. 1948 Loup doun ; or, be the gude Lord ! thow sall los
 thy heid.

PAVPER.

I sal anis drink, or I ga, thocht thou had sworne my deid.

I will drink before I go, any way.

(*Heir Diligence castis away the ledder.*)

DILIGENCE.

Loup now, gif thou list; for thou hes lost the ledder.

Now you may jump down.

PAVPER.

It is, full weil, thy kind to loup and licht in a ledder.

1952 Thou sal be faine to fetch agane ȝe ledder, or I loup.

I sall sit heir, into this tcheir, till I haue tumde the stoup.

Jumping into a halter is like you.

I will sit here till I have emptied the pitcher.

(*Heir sall the Carle loup aff the scaffald.*)

Swyith ! begger ! bogill ! haist the away !
Thow art over pert to spill our play.

Go! Don't spoil our play.

PAVPER.

1956 I wil not gif, for al ȝour play, worth an sowis fart ;
For thair is richt lytill play at my hungrie hart.

Bother your play ! I am hungry.

DILIGENCE.

Quhat Devill ails this cruckit carle ?

What ails the fellow ?

PAVPER.

Marie ! Meikill sorrow.
1960 I can not get, thocht I gasp, to beg, nor to borrow.

I am in great grief. I can neither beg nor borrow.

DILIGENCE.

Quhair deuill is this thou dwels ? Or quhats thy intent ?

Where do you live ? And what do you want ?

PAVPER.

I dwell into Lawthiane, ane myle fra Tranent.

I live in Lothian, near Tranent.

ANE SATYRE.

DILIGENCE.

Where would
you go, really?

Quhair wald thou be, carle? The suth to me
schaw.

PAVPER.

To S. Andrews,
for justice.

1964 Sir, evin to Sanct-Androes, for to seik law.

DILIGENCE.

Edinburgh is the
place for that.

For to seik law, in Edinburgh was the neirest
way.

PAVPER.

I could get none

there, Devil

take the crew!

1968

Sir, I socht law thair this monie deir day;
Bot I culd get nane at Sessioun nor Sein3e :
Thairfoir, the mekill din Deuill droun all the
mein3e!

DILIGENCE.

Explain to me,

in full, how you

have come to

this condition.

Shaw me thy mater, man, with al the circum-
stances,
How that thou hes happinit on thir vnhappie
chances.

PAVPER.

I will declare

the black truth.

My father was
eighty and more;
my mother,
ninety-five.

I supported them.

We had a
mare that
foaled yearly;

and three cows,

of the best.

My father died;

and my mother

mourned bitterly.

1972

1976

1980

Gude-man, will 3e gif me 3our Charitie,
And I sall declair 3ow the black veritie.
My father was ane auld man, and ane hoir,
And was of age fourscoir of 3eirs and moir;
And Mald, my mother, was fourscoir and fyfteine;
And with my labour I did thame baith susteine.
Wee had ane Meir, that caryit salt and coill;
And everie ilk 3eir scho brocht vs hame ane foill.
Wee had thrie ky, that was baith fat and fair,—
Nane tydier into the toun of Air.
My father was sa waik of blude and bane,
That he deit; quhairfoir my mother maid great
maine.

Then scho deit, within ane day or two ; *Then she died,*

1984 And thair began my povertie and wo. *to my misery.*

Our gude gray Meir was baittand on the feild ; *The mare went*

And our Lands laird tuik hir for his hyreild. *for heriot.*

The Vickar tuik the best Cow be the head, *The vicar took*

1988 Incontinent, quhen my father was deid ; *one cow, on my*

And, quhen the Vickar hard tel how that my *father's death,*

mother *and another, on*

Was dead, fra-hand he tuke to him ane vther. *my mother's.*

Then Meg, my wife, did murne, both evin & *Next, Meg, my*

morow, *wife, grieved*

1992 Till, at the last, scho deit for verie sorow. *to death ;*

And, quhen the Vickar hard tell my wyfe was *and then the*

dead, *vicar took the*

The thrid Cow he cleikit be the head. *third cow.*

Thair vmest clayis, that was of rapploch gray, *The vicar's clerk,*

1996 The Vickar gart his Clark bear them away. *too, got spoil.*

Quhen all was gaine, I micht mak na debeat, *At this I was*

Bot, with my bairns, past for till beg my meat. *driven to beg.*

Now haue I tald ȝow the blak veritie, *Thus, in truth,*

was I brought

2000 How I am brocht into this miserie. *to this.*

DILIGENCE.

How did ȝe person ? Was he not thy gude freind ? *But the parson was your friend?*

PAVPER.

The devil stick him ! He curst me for my teind, *He excommuni-*

And halds me ȝit vnder that same proces, *cated me for not*

2004 That gart me want the Sacrament at Pasche. *paying my tithes.*

In gude faith, sir, thocht he wald cut my throt, *I have only a*

groat left, with

I haue na geir except ane Inglis grot, *which I mean to*

Quhilk I purpois to gif ane man of law. *fee a lawyer.*

DILIGENCE.

2008 Thou art the daftest fuill that ever I saw. *You are a great fool, if you hope*

Trows thou, man, be the law to get remeid *to get anything from priests*

Of men of kirk ? Na, nocht till thou be deid. *by law.*

PAVPER.

By what law may
a vicar take three
cows from me ?

2012

Sir, be quhat law, tell me, quhairfoir, or quhy,

That ane Vickar sould tak fra me thrie ky.

DILIGENCE.

Use in law

enough for such.

Thay haue na law exceptand consuetude,

Quhilk law, to them, is sufficient and gude.

PAVPER.

Such use should

not be law.

2016

And where is a

law to be found,

to rob me of

three cows ?

2020

Ane consuetude against the common weill

Sould be na law, I think, be sweit Sanct Geill !

Quhair will ȝe find that law, tell, gif ȝe can,

To tak thrie ky fra ane pure husband man ;

Ane for my father, and for my wyfe ane vther,

And the thrid Cow he tuke fra Mald, my mother.

DILIGENCE.

This is

priests' law.

It is thair law, all that thay haue in vse,

Thocht it be Cow, Sow, Ganer, Gryse, or Guse.

PAVPER.

Certain prelates

of these parts

are in use to

make free with

womankind.

Is this law

bad, or good ?

2024

2028

Sir, I wald speir at ȝow ane questioun.

Behauld sum Prelats of this Regioun :

Manifestlie, during thair lustie lyfis,

Thay swyfe Ladies, Madinis, and vther mens

wyfis ;

And sa thair cunts thay haue in consuetude.

Quhidder say ȝe that law is evill, or gude ?

DILIGENCE.

Be quiet ! You

must be mad.

There is peril
in speaking
thus of priests.

Hald thy toung, man ! It seims that thou war

mangit.

Speik thou of Preists, but doubt thou will be

hangit.

PAVPER.

Perils I

heed nothing.

2032

Be him that buir the cruell Croun of thorne !

I cair nocht to be hangit evin the morne.

DILIGENCE.

Be sure, of Preistis thou will get na support.

PAVPER.

Gif that be trew, the feind resaue the sort !

Sa, sen I se I get na vther grace,

2036   I will ly doun, and rest mee in this place.

(Pauper lyis doun in the feild. Pardoner enters.)

PARDONER.

Bona dies ! Bona dies !

Devoit peopill, gude day I say ȝow.

Now tarie ane lytill quhyll, I pray ȝow,

2040   Till I be with ȝow knawin.

Wait ȝe weill how I am namit ?

Ane nobill man, and vndefamit,

    Gif all the suith war schawin.

2044   I am sir Robert Rome-raker,

Ane perfite publike pardoner,

    Admittit be the Paip.

Sirs, I sall schaw ȝow, for my wage,

2048   My pardons and my pilgramage,

    Quhilk ȝe sall se and graip.

I giue to the deuill, with gude intent,

This vnsell wickit New-testament,

2052   With them that it translaitit.

Sen layik men knew the veritie,

Pardoners gets no charitie,

    Without that thay debait it

2056   Amang the wiues, with wrinks and wyles,

As all my marrowis men begyles

    With our fair fals flattrie.

ȝea, all the crafts I ken perqueir,

2060   As I was teichit be ane Freir

    Callit Hypocrisic.

Bot now, allace ! our greit abusioun

it is hard times with us.	Is cleirlie knawin, till our confusioun,
	2064 That we may sair repent.
My credit is spoilt by knowledge of the New Testament.	Of all credence now I am quyte; For ilk man halds me at dispyte, That reids the New-test'ment.
Renewed	2068 Duill fell the braine that hes it wrocht!
cursing.	Sa fall them that the Buik hame brocht!
Would that Luther and the rest had been smothered by their chrisom-cloths!	Als, I pray to the Rude, That Martin Luther, that fals loun, 2072 Black Bullinger, and Melancthoun Had bene smorde in their cude.
As to S. Paul, I wish he had never been born; and I wish his books were kept out of sight, or else torn up.	Be him that buir the crowne of thorne! I wald Sanct Paull had neuer bene borne; 2076 And, als, I wald his buiks War never red into the kirk, Bot amangs freirs, into the mirk, Or riuen amang ruiks.

(Heir sall he lay doun his geir vpon ane buird, and say :)

Come and see my patent pardons.	2080 My patent pardouns ʒe may se, Cum fra the Caue of Tartarie, Weill seald with oster-schellis.
Even without repentance you shall have full pardon.	Thocht ʒe haue na contritioun, 2084 ʒe sall haue full remissioun, With help of Buiks and bellis.
Here is a prime relic of a man;	Heir is ane relict, lang and braid, Of Fine Macoull the richt chaft blaid, 2088 With teith and al togidder.
and here is one of a peccant beast.	Of Collings cow heir is ane horne; For eating of Makconnals corne, Was slaine into Baquhidder.
Here, too, is the cord that throttled John Armstrong:	2092 Heir is ane coird, baith great and lang,— Quhilk hangit Johne the Armistrang,— Of gude hemp, soft and sound.
whoso is hanged with it need never be drowned.	Gude, halie peopill, I stand for'd, 2096 Quha ever beis hangit with this cord Neids never to be dround.

The culum of Sanct Bryds kow ;

The gruntill of Sanct Antonis sow,

2100   Quhilk buir his haly bell.

Quhaever he be heiris this bell clinck,—

Gif me ane ducat for till drink,—

He sall never gang to hell,

2104 Without he be of Baliell borne.

Maisters, trow ȝe that this be scorne ?

      Cum, win this pardoun : cum.

Quha luifis thair wyfis nocht with thair hart,

2108 I haue power them for till part.

      Me think ȝow deif and dum.

Hes naine of ȝow curst wickit wyfis,

That halds ȝow into sturt and stryfis ?

2112   Cum, tak my dispensatioun.

Of that cummer I sall mak ȝow quyte,

Howbeit ȝour selfis be in the wyte,

      And mak ane fals narratioun.

2116 Cum, win the pardoun,—now let se,—

For meill, for malt, or for monie,

      For cok, hen, guse, or gryse.

Of relicts heir I haue ane hunder.

2120 Quhy cum ȝe nocht ?   This is ane wonder.

      I trow ȝe be nocht wyse.

SOWTAR.

Welcum hame, Robert Rome-raker,

Our halie, patent pardoner !

2124   Gif ȝe haue dispensatioun

To pairt me and my wickit wyfe,

And me deliver from sturt and stryfe,

      I mak ȝow supplicatioun.

PARDONER.

2128 I sall ȝow pairt but mair demand,

Sa I get mony in my hand.

      Thairfoir, let se sum cunȝe.

6

Side notes:

See S. Bride's cow's tail, and S. Antony's sow's snout.

He who hears this bell—I wager a ducat,—will never go to hell, unless born of Belial.

Have a pardon.

I can part ill-assorted couples.

If any of you has a troublesome wife, I can relieve him of her,

though he may be in the wrong and may lie.

I take anything in payment.

My relics you are fools to despise.

Welcome home, pardoner !

If you can separate me and my wicked wife, I pray you to help me.

I will do it for money. Show your coin.

ANE SATYRE.

SOWTAR.

I have only five
shillings; but
they shall
be yours.

2132

I haue na silver,—be my lyfe !—
Bot fyue schillings, and my schaipping knyfe.
That sall ȝe haue, but sunȝe.

PARDONER.

What is your
wife like ?

Quhat kynd of woman is thy wyfe ?

SOWTAR.

Quarrelsome,

filthy,

violent,

altogether

disagreeable.

She vexes me all

day, and scolds

my sleep away.

The Devil himself

could not abide

the horror.

2136

2140

2144

Ane quick Devill, Sir ; ane storme of stryfe ;
Ane Frog that fyles the winde ;
Ane fistand flag ; a flagartie fuffe :
At ilk ane pant scho lets ane puffe,
And hes na ho behind.
All the lang day scho me dispyts ;
And all the nicht scho flings and flyts,
Thus sleip I never ane wink.
That Cockatrice, that commoun huir,
The mekill Devill may nocht induir
Hir stuburnnes and stink.

SOWTARS WIFE.

I hear you, thief;
and you shall
smart, when I
lay hold of you.

2148

Theif ! carle ! thy words I hard rycht weill.
In faith, my freindschip ȝe sall feill,
And I the fang.

SOWTAR.

If I did not

praise you, may

I swing for it !

Gif I said ocht, Dame,—be the Rude !—
Except ȝe war baith fair and gude,
God ! nor I hang !

PARDONER.

Dame, I can part

you and him.

Do you consent ?

2152

Fair dame, gif ȝe wald be ane wower,
To part ȝow twa I haue ane power.
Tell on. Ar ȝe content ?

SOWTARS WYFE.

3e, that I am, with all my hart,   Mo.st heartily,
2156 Fra that fals huirsone till depart,   if this thief
    Gif this theif will consent.   will.
Causses to part I haue anew ;   I have a
Becaus I gat na chamber-glew.   wife's good
2160   I tell 3ow, verely,   reasons ;
I meruell nocht sa mot I lyfe ;   for this drone
Howbeit that swingeour can not swyfe,   is no husband
    He is baith cauld and dry.   to poor me.

PARDONER.

2164 Quhat wil 3e gif me, for 3our part ?   What will
                  you give ?

SOWTARS WYFE.

Ane cuppill of sarks, with all my hart,   Two shifts, of the
    The best claith in the land.   best of stuff.

PARDONER.

To part sen 3e ar baith content,   I will separate
2168 I sall 3ow part incontinent :   you, if you do
    Bot 3e mon do command.   my bidding.
My will and finall sentence is,   My sentence
Ilk ane of 3ow vthers arsse kis.   is, that you
2172 Slip doun 3our hois. Me thinkis the carle is   kiss each other.
    glaikit.   Dame, do you
Set thou not by, howbeit scho kisse and slaik it.   kiss first.
   (*Heir sall scho kis his arsse with silence.*)
Lift vp hir clais : kis hir hoill with 3our hart.   And now kiss her.

SOWTAR.

I pray 3ow, sir, forbid hir for to fart.   But make terms
   (*Heir sall the Carle kis hir arsse with silence.*)   with her.

PARDONER.

2176 Dame, pas.3e to the east end of the toun ;   Now one will go
    And pas 3e west, evin lyke ane cuckald loun.   east, and the
                  other will
                  go west.

Away, both!
How glad
they are!

Go hence, ʒe baith, with Baliels braid blissing
Schirs, saw ʒe ever mair sorrowles pairting?

(Heir sall the boy cry aff the hill.)

WILKIN.

Where are you? 2180 Hoaw! maister, hoaw! quhair ar ʒe now?

PARDONER.

Here, rascal. I am heir, Wilkin, widdiefow.

WILKIN.

I have obeyed
you, and have
found a horse-
bean on Dame
Flesher's dung-
hill.

Sir, I haue done ʒour bidding;
For I haue fund ane great hors-bane—
2184 Ane fairer saw ʒe never nane,—
      Vpon Dame Fleschers midding.

You may per-
suade the women
it is good
against fever.

Sir, ʒe may gar the wyfis trow
It is ane bane of Sanct Bryds cow,
2188   Gude for the feuer quartane.

Be wary, now,
and you will have
them at your will,
far and near.

Sir, will ʒe reull this relict weill,
All the wyfis will baith kis and kneill,
      Betuixt this and Dumbartane.

PARDONER.

What is said
of me? 2192 Quhat say thay of me in the toun?

WILKIN.

Your reputation
is very good with
a few, but exceed-
ingly bad with
the majority.

Sum sayis ʒe ar ane verie loun;
      Sum sayis Legatus natus;
Sum sayis ʒ'ar ane fals Saracene;
2196 And sum sayis ʒe ar, for certaine,
      Diabolus incarnatus.

Keep out of the
power of King
Correction,
however; or,
being what you
are, you will
assuredly
be hanged.

Bot keip ʒow fra subiectioun
Of the curst King Correctioun;
2200   For, be ʒe with him fangit,
Becaus ʒe ar ane Rome-raker,
Ane commoun, publick cawsay-paker,
      But doubt ʒe will be hangit.

88

PARDONER.

2204 Quhair sall I ludge into the toun ?

Where shall I lodge ?

WILKIN.

With gude, kynde Christiane Anderson,
Quhair ʒe will be weill treatit.
Gif ony limmer ʒow demands,
2208 Scho will defend ʒow with hir hands,
And womanlie debait it.
Bawburdie says, be the Trinitie !
That scho sall beir ʒow cumpanie,
2212 Howbeit ʒe byde ane ʒeir.

Christiane Anderson will treat you well, and will defend you as a woman can.

Bawburdie says she will bear you company, though you stay a year.

PARDONER.

Thou hes done weill, be Gods mother !
Tak ʒe the taine, and I the t'other ;
Sa sall we mak greit cheir.

Well done! Each taking one, we shall fare bravely.

WILKIN.

2216 I reid ʒow, speid ʒow heir,
And mak na langer tarie.
Byde ʒe lang thair, but weir
I dreid ʒour weird ʒow warie.

Don't delay any longer ; or it will not be good for you.

(*Heir sall Pauper rise and rax him.*)

PAVPER.

2220 Quhat thing was ʒon that I hard crak & cry ?
I haue bene dreamand and dreueland of my ky.
With my richt hand my haill bodie I saine :
Sanct Bryd, Sanct Bryd, send me my ky againe !
2224 I se standand ʒonder ane halie man :
To mak me help let me se gif he can.
Halie maister, God speid ʒow ! and gude morne !

I have been dreaming of my cow.

Send her to me, S. Bride!

Can yonder holy man help me ?

Good morrow! sir.

PARDONER.

Welcum to me, thocht thou war at the horne.
2228 Cum, win the pardoun ; and syne I sall the saine.

Welcome!

Have a pardon.

89

PAVPER.

Will it restore
my cow?

Wil that pardoun get me my ky againe ?

PARDONER.

I ask if you will
have a pardon.

Carle, of thy ky I haue nathing ado.
Cum, win my pardon ; and kis my relicts, to.

(*Heir sall he saine him with his relictis.*)

Untie your
purse, and
have a pardon.

2232　Now lows thy pursse, & lay doun thy offrand,
And thou sall haue my pardon, euin fra hand.

I can bless away
all your ailments.

With raipis and relicts I sall the saine againe ;
Of Gut or grauell thou sall neuer haue paine.

Have a pardon.

2236　Now win the pardon, limmer ; or thou art lost.

PAVPER.

What will it cost ?

My haly father, quhat wil that pardon cost ?

PARDONER.

What money
have you ?

Let se quhat mony thou bearest in thy bag.

PAVPER.

A groat.

I haue ane grot heir, bund into ane rag.

PARDONER.

No more silver ?

2240　Hes thou na vther siluer bot ane groat ?

PAVPER.

Search me.

Gif I haue mair, sir, cum and rype my coat.

PARDONER.

Give me
that, then.

Gif me that grot, man, gif thou hest na mair.

PAVPER.

I will. And now
for the pardon.

With all my heart, maister.　Lo ! tak it thair.

2244　Now let me se ȝour pardon, with ȝour leif.

PARDONER.

I pardon you for a
thousand years.

Ane thousand ȝeir of pardons I the geif.

PAVPER.

Ane thousand ʒeir ? I will not liuè sa lang.
Delyuer me it, maister, and let me gang.

I shan't live so long. Give me the pardon.

PARDONER.

2248 Ane thousand ʒeir I lay vpon thy head,
With totiens quotiens. Now mak me na mair
plead.
Thou hast resaifit thy pardon now already.

For a thousand years. And now enough !

PAVPER.

Bot I can se na thing, sir, be our Lady !
2252 Forsuith, maister, I trow I be not wyse,
To pay ere I haue sene my marchandryse.
That ʒe haue gottin my groat full sair I rew.
Sir, quhidder is ʒour pardon black, or blew ?
2256 Maister, sen ʒe haue taine fra me my cunʒie,
My marchandryse schaw me, withouttin sunʒie ;
Or to the Bischop I sall pas, and pleinʒie
In Sanct-Androis, & summond ʒow to the Seinʒie.

I see nothing; money gone, and no wares, to my grief! Show me what you give me for my coin; or I will complain of you.

PARDONER.

2260 Quhat craifis the carle ? Me thinks thou art not
wise.

The fellow must be silly.

PAVPER.

I craif my groat, or ellis my marchandrise.

My groat, or something for it :

PARDONER.

I gaif the pardon for ane thowsand ʒeir.

I pardoned you for a thousand years.

PAVPER.

How sall I get that pardon, let me heir.

How shall I get the pardon ?

PARDONER.

2264 Stand still, and I sall tell the haill storie.
Quhen thow art deid, and gais to Purgatorie,

When you die, and go to Purgatory,

to be tormented
a thousand years,
the pardon will
relieve you.Being condempit to paine a thowsand ʒeir,
Then sall thy pardoun the releif, but weir.
2268 Now be content. ʒe ar ane mervelous man.

PAVPER.

Shall I get no-
thing the while?Sall I get nathing for my grot quhill than?

PARDONER.

No, to be plain.That sall thou not, I mak it to ʒow plaine.

PAVPER.

Then give
me back my
groat;
for you don't
bargain
fairly.
When I die, I

must go to

Purgatory.
But tell me where
I shall find you.
In hell, where
you can't
help yourself.
Before you helped
me, I should
get scorched.
Do you think
I will buy
blind lambs?
Give me back
my groat.Na? Than, gossop, gif me my grot againe.
2272 Quhat say ʒe, maisters? Call ʒe this gude
          resoun,
That he sould promeis me ane gay pardoun,
And he resaue my money in his stead,
Syne mak me na payment till I be dead?
2276 Quhen I am deid, I wait full sikkerlie,
My sillie saull will pas to Purgatorie.
Declair me this:—Now God nor Baliell bind
          the!—
Quhen I am thair, curst carle, quhair sall I find
          the?
2280 Not into heavin, bot, rather, into hell.
Quhen *th*ou are thair, thou can not help thy sel.
Quhen will thou cum my dolours till abait,
Or I the find, my hippis will get ane hait.
2284 Trowis thou, butchour, that I will by blind
          lambis?
Gif me my grot. The devill dryte in thy gambis!

PARDONER.

He must be mad.

You don't get
your groat again.Suyith! stand abak! I trow this man be mangit.
Thou gets not this, carle, thocht *th*ou suld be
          hangit.

92

PAVPER.

2288   Gif me my grot, weill bund into ane clout ;
       Or, be Gods breid ! Robin sall beir ane rout.

Give me my groat; or you shall be thrashed.

(Heir sal thay fecht with silence ; and Pauper sal cast doun the buird, and cast the relicts in the water.)

DILIGENCE.

    Quhat kind of daffing is this al day ?
    Suyith ! smaiks, out of the feild ! away !

What fooling is this ? Away !

2292   Into ane presoun put them sone ;
       Syne hang them, quhen the play is done.

Shut them up; and hang them, when the play is over.

      (Heir sall Diligence mak his proclamatioun.)

    Famous peopill, tak tent, and ȝe sall se
    The thrie estaits of this natioun

The three Estates are coming to Court, with strange gravity.

2296   Cum to the Court, with ane strange gravitie.
       Thairfoir, I mak ȝow supplicatioun,

Be silent, then,

    Till ȝe haue heard our haill narratioun,

I pray you, till

    To keip silence and be patient, I pray ȝow.

I have told all.

2300   Howbeit we speik be adulatioun,

I shall speak

       Wee sall say nathing bot the suith, I say ȝow.

the truth only.

    Gude, verteous men, that luifis the veritie,
    I wait thay will excuse our negligence.

The virtuous will make allowance.

2304   Bot vicious men, denude of charitie,
       As feinȝeit, fals, flattrand Saracens,

As to the vicious, uncharitable, they will cry venge- ance on us : but we must have patience, and refer ourselves to the faithful.

    Howbeit thay cry on vs ane loud vengence,
    And of our pastyme mak ane fals report,

2308   Quhat may wee do bot tak in patience,
       And vs refer vnto the faithfull sort ?

    Our Lord Jesus, Peter, nor Paull

Even Christ and

    Culd nocht compleis the peopill all ;

the Saints could

2312   Bot sum war miscontent.

not please all.

    Howbeit thay schew the veritie,

Though they showed the truth, some denounced it.

    Sum said that it war heresie,
      Be thair maist fals iudgement.

(Heir sall the thrie estaits cum fra the palȝeoun, gangand back- wart, led be thair vyces.)

WANTONNES.

What is that
I see?
Look, Solace!

2316   Now, braid benedicite !
        Quhat thing is ȝon that I se ?
        Luke, Solace, my hart !

SOLACE.

What think you?

The three
Estates, march-
ing backwards.

        Brother Wantonnes, quhat thinks thow ?
2320   Ȝon ar the thrie estaits, I trow,
        Gangand backwart.

WANTONNES.

Backwards?

It is a shame
they should
march so.

Correction

must soon

effect a reform.

Let us tell
the King.

        Backwart, backwart ?   Out ! Wallaway !
        It is greit schame for them, I say,
2324   Backwart to gang.
        I trow the King Correctioun
        Man mak ane reformatioun,
            Or it be lang.
2328 · Now let vs go and tell the King.

                    (*Pausa.*)

Sire, we have seen

a strange thing,—

the three Estates
proceeding to
Parliament
backwards.

        Sir, wee haue sene ane mervelous thing,
            Be our iudgement :
        The thrie estaits of this Regioun
2332   Ar cummand backwart, throw this toun,
            To the Parlament.

REX HVMANITAS.

Indeed?

Send them to
me, lest they
go wrong.

        Backwart, backwart ?   How may that be ?
        Gar speid them haistelie to me,
2336   In dreid that thay ga wrang.

PLACEBO.

They will get
here as fast
as their speed
will let them.

        Sir, I se them ȝonder cummand.
        Thay will be heir evin fra hand,
            Als fast as thay may gang.

GVDE-COUNSELL.

2340 Sir, hald ȝou stil, & skar them nocht,
 Till ȝe persaue quhat be thair thocht,
  And se quhat men them leids ;
 And let the King Correctioun
2344 Mak ane scharp inquisitioun,
  And mark them be the heids.
 Quhen ȝe ken the occasioun
 That maks them sic persuasioun,
2348 ȝe may expell the caus ;
 Syne, them reforme, as ȝe think best,
 Sua that the Realme may liue in rest,
  According to Gods lawis.

Don't alarm them, till we learn their intent and their leaders; and let King Correction observe them narrowly. First, we must find out the cause of this procedure; and then they may be reformed, and the realm may live in peace.

(*Heir sall the thrie estaits cum, and turne thair faces to the King.*)

SPIRITVALITIE.

2352 Gloir, honour, laud, triumph, and victorie
 Be to ȝour michtie prudent excellence !
 Heir ar we cum, all the estaits thrie,
 Readie to mak our dew obedience,
2356 At ȝour command, with humbill observance,
 As may pertene to Spiritualitie,
 With counsell of the Temporalitie.

All hail to your Excelleney ! We come to make our obedience, at your command, with advice of the Temporalty.

TEMPORALITIE.

 Sir, we, with michtie curage, at command
2360 Of ȝour superexcellent Maiestie,
 Sall mak seruice baith with our hart and hand,
 And sall not dreid in thy defence to die.
 Wee ar content, but doubt, that wee may se
2364 That nobill, heavinlie King Correctioun,
 Sa he with mercie mak punitioun.

Sire, at your command, we will make service, even with our lives. King Correction is welcome, so he punish with mercy.

MERCHAND.

 Sir, we ar heir, ȝour Burgessis and Merchands.
 Thanks be to God that we may se ȝour face,

We, burgesses and merchants, welcome you,

2368 Traistand wee may, now, into divers lands
      Convoy our geir, with support of ʒour grace ;
      For now, I traist, wee sall get rest and peace.
      Quhen misdoars ar with ʒour sword overthrawin,
2372 Then may leil merchands liue vpon thair awin.

REX HVMANITAS.

      Welcum to me, my prudent Lords, all !
      ʒe ar my members, suppois I be ʒour head.
      Sit doun, that we may, with ʒour iust counsall,
2376 Aganis misdoars find soveraine remeid.
      Wee sall nocht spair, for fauour nor for feid,
      With ʒour avice, to mak punitioun,
      And put my sword to executioun.

CORRECTIOVN.

2380 My tender freinds, I pray ʒow, with my hart,
      Declair to me the thing that I wald speir.
      Quhat is the caus that ʒe gang, all, backwart ?
      The veritie thairof faine wald I heir.

SPIRITVALITIE.

2384 Soveraine, we haue gaine sa this mony a ʒeir.
      Howbeit ʒe think we go vndecently,
      Wee think wee gang richt wonder pleasantly.

DILIGENCE.

      Sit doun, my Lords, into ʒour proper places ;
2388 Syne, let the King consider all sic caces.
      Sit doun, sir scribe, and sit doun, dampster, to ;
      And fence the Court, as ʒe war wont to do.

      (*Thay ar set doun ; & Gud-Counsell sal pas to his seat.*)

REX HVMANITAS.

      My prudent Lords of the thrie estaits,
2392 It is our will, abuife all vther thing,

For to reforme all them that maks debaits   to take order for
Contrair the richt, quhilk daylie dois maling,   the better ruling
And thay that dois the Common-weil doun   of the common-
thring.   wealth.

2396 With help and counsell of King Correctioun,   King Correction
It is our will for to mak punisching,   aiding us, we
And plaine oppressours put to subiectioun.   will do away
                                                   with oppression.

SPIRITVALITIE.

Quhat thing is this, sir, that ȝe haue devysit?   You must
2400 Schirs, ȝe haue neid for till be weill advysit. be cautious,
Be nocht haistie into ȝour execution ;   Avoid haste
And be nocht ouir extreime in ȝour punitioun :   and severity.
And, gif ȝe please to do, sir, as wee say,   We counsel
2404 Postpone this Parlament till ane vther day.   adjournment;
For quhy the peopill of this Regioun   for the people
May nocht indure extreme correctioun.   cannot endure
                                                   extreme
                                                   correction.

CORRECTIOVN.

Is this the part, my Lords, that ȝe will tak   Do you thus
2408 To mak vs supportatioun to correct ?   further our
                                                   reform ?
It dois appeir that ȝe ar culpabill,   You must, indeed,
That ar nocht to Correctioun applyabill.   be in fault.
Suyith ! Diligence. Ga schaw it is our will   Diligence, let
2412 That everilk man opprest geif in his Bill.   all complain
                                                   that would.

DILIGENCE.

All maneir of men I wairne, that be opprest,   All shall have
Cum and complaine, and thay salbe redrest ;   justice, if they
                                                   apply for it;
For quhy it is the nobill Princes will,   and such is the
2416 That ilk compleiner sall gif in his Bill.   will of the Prince.

IOHNE THE COMMON-WEILL.

Out of my gait ! For Gods saik, let me ga !   Stand aside !
Tell me againe, gude maister, quhat ȝe say.   Repeat that.

DILIGENCE.

2420

I warne al that be wrangouslie offendit,
Cum and complaine, and thay sall be amendit.

IOHNE.

Thankit be Christ, *that* buir the croun of thorne !
For I was never sa blyth sen I was borne.

DILIGENCE.

Quhat is thy name, fallow ? That wald I feil.

IOHNE.

2424

Forsuith, thay call me Iohne the common-weil.
Gude maister, I wald speir at ȝou ane thing :
Quhair traist ȝe I sall find ȝon new-cumde King ?

DILIGENCE.

Cum over, and I sall schaw the to his grace.

IOHNE.

2428

Gods bennesone licht on that luckie face !
Stand by the gait : let se gif I can loup.
I man rin fast, in cace I get ane coup.

(*Heir sall Iohne loup the stank, or els fall in it.*)

DILIGENCE.

Speid the away. Thou taryis all to lang.

IOHNE.

2432

Now be this day I may na faster gang.

IOHNE TO THE KING.

Gude day, gud day ! Grit God saif baith ȝour
graces !
Wallie, wallie fall thay twa weill-fairde faces !

REX HVMANITAS.

Shaw me thy name, gude man, I the command.

IOHNE.

2436 Marie! Iohne, the common-weil of fair Scotland.

John the Commonwealth.

REX HVMANITAS.

The commoun-weill hes bene amang his fais.

The Commonwealth was among his enemies.

IOHNE.

ȝe, sir. . That gars the commoun-weil want clais.

So he had no clothes.

REX HVMANITAS.

Quhat is the caus the common-weil is crukit ?

Why is the Commonwealth lame ?

IOHNE.

2440 Becaus the common-weill hes bene overlukit.

From being neglected.

REX HVMANITAS.

Quhat gars the luke sa with ane dreirie hart ?

Why look you so sad ?

IOHNE.

Becaus the thrie estaits gangs, all, backwart.

Because the three Estates go backwards.

REX HVMANITAS.

Sir common-weill, knaw ȝe the limmers that
    them leids?

Do you know the rogues that lead them ?

IOHNE.

2444 Thair canker cullours, I ken them be the heads.
As for our reverent fathers of Spiritualitie,
Thay ar led be Couetice and cairles Sensualitie ;
And, as ȝe se, Temporalitie hes neid of correctioun,
2448 Quhilk hes, lang tyme, bene led be publick
    oppressioun.
Loe, quhair the loun lyis lurkand at his back !
Get vp! I think to se thy craig gar ane raip crack.
Loe ! heir is Falset and Dissait, weill I ken,
2452 Leiders of the merchants and sillie crafts-men.
Quhat mervell thocht the thrie estaits backwart
    gang,

I know them,—
the leaders of the
Spirituality,
and also the
leader of the
Temporalty.
For him a
rope were fit.
And I know
others' leaders.
What wonder,
if the three
Estates march

Quhen sic an vyle cumpanie dwels them amang,

backwards,

Quhilk hes reulit this rout monie deir dayis,

and that I, for

2456 Quhilk gars Iohn the common-weil want his

my part, want

warme clais !

warm clothes !

Sir, call them befoir ʒow, and put them in ordour;

Reform them;

Or els Iohn the common-weil man beg on the

or else I

bordour.

must beg.

Thou feinʒeit Flattrie, the feind fart in thy face !

As to Flattery,—

2460 Quhen ʒe was guyder of the Court, we gat litill

who defrauded

grace.

us,—

Ryse vp, Falset and Dissait, without ony sunʒe.

and Falsehood

I pray God, nor the devils dame dryte on thy

and Deceit,

grunʒe !

I curse them.

Behauld as the loun lukis evin lyke a thief.

Much harm has

2464 Monie wicht warkman thou brocht to mischief.

been wrought.

My soveraine, Lord Correctioun, I mak ʒow sup-

Lord Correction,

plication,

I pray you to

Put thir tryit truikers from Christis congrega-

excommunicate

tion.

all three.

CORRECTIOUN.

As ʒe haue devysit, but doubt it salbe done.

Be it so.

2468 Cum heir, my Sergeants, and do ʒour debt sone.

Serjeants, im-
prison these
thieves. Hang-
ing would be
none too much
for them.

Put thir thrie pellours into pressoun strang.

Howbeit ʒe sould hang them, ʒe do them na

wrang.

FIRST SERGEANT.

Soverane Lords, wee sall obey ʒour commands.

We obey.

2472 Brother, vpon thir limmers lay on thy hands.

Help, brother !

Ryse vp sone, loun ! Thou luiks evin lyke ane

Get up, you

lurden.

vile-looking

ʒour mouth war meit to drink an wesche iurden.

miscreant !

SECVND SERGEANT.

Cum heir, gossop ; cum heir, cum heir.

You shall repent

2476 ʒour rackles lyfe ʒe sall repent.

your past life.

100

Quhen was ʒe wont to be sa sweir?
Stand still, and be obedient.

Lazy now?
Obey me.

FIRST SERGEANT.

Thair is nocht, in all this toun,—
2480 Bot I wald nocht this taill war tald,—
Bot I wald hang him for his goun,
Quhidder that it war Laird or laid.
I trow this pellour be spur-gaid.
2484 Put in thy hand into this cord.
Howbeit I se thy skap skyre skaid,
Thou art ane stewat, I stand foird.

Confidentially,
I would hang
any one here,
high or low,
for his gown.
Mind what I say,

you spur-galled,

scabby stinkard.

(*Heir sall the vycis be led to the stocks.*)

SECVND SERGEANT.

Put in ʒour leggis into the stocks;
2488 For ʒe had never ane meiter hois.
Thir stewats stinks as thay war Broks.
Now ar ʒe sikker, I suppois.

The stocks
fit you well.
What nosegays.·
Now you are safe.

(*Pausa.*)

My Lords, wee haue done ʒour commands.
2492 Sall wee put Covetice in captivitie?

Shall we shut up
Covetousness?

CORRECTIOVN.

ʒe: hardlie lay on them ʒour hands;
Rycht sa, vpon Sensualitie.

Just so; and
Sensuality.

SPIRITVALITIE.

Thir is my Grainter and my Chalmerlaine,
2496 And hes my gould and geir vnder thair cuiris.
I mak ane vow to God, I sall complaine
Vnto the Paip how ʒe do me iniuris.

These are my
general wardens.
I will complain
to the Pope.

COVETICE.

My reverent fathers, tak in patience.
2500 I sall nocht lang remaine from ʒour presence.

Fathers, I will
soon return.

7

Meanwhile
my spirit remains
with you;
Thocht for ane quhyll I man from ʒow depairt,
I wait my spreit sall remaine in ʒour hart ;

and, Correction
gone, we shall
both come back.
And, quhen this King Correctioun beis absent,

2504   Then sall we twa returne incontinent.

Adieu !
Thairfoir, adew !

SPIRITVALITIE.

Adieu ! We assert

naturally.
Adew ! be Sanct Mavene !
Pas quhair ʒe will, we ar twa naturall men.

SENSVALITIE.

Adieu !   2508   Adew ! my Lord.

SPIRITVALITIE.

Adieu ! Alas
that we
must part !
Adew ! my awin sweit hart.
Now duill fell me, that wee twa man depart.

SENSVALITIE.

I trust we shall
soon come
together again.
My Lord, howbeit this parting dois me paine,

2512   I traist in God we sal meit sone agane.

SPIRITVALITIE.

Hasten back.
You are
indispensable.
To cum againe, I pray ʒow, do ʒour cure.
Want I ʒow twa, I may nocht lang indure.

(*Heir sal the Sergeants chase them away ; and they sal gang to
the seat of Sensualitie.*)

TEMPORALITIE.

The Estates
should strive for
Commonwealth.
My Lords, ʒe knaw the thrie estaits

2516   For Common-weill suld mak debaits.

So let us concert
Let, now, amang vs, be devysit

to this end, con-
Sic actis that with gude men be praysit,

forming to the
Conforming to the common law ;

common law,   2520   For of na man we sould stand aw.

and using the aid
of Good Counsel
versed in the
canon law and
the civil.
And, for till saif vs fra murmell,
Schone, Diligence, fetch vs Gude-counsell ;
For quhy he is ane man that knawis

2524   Baith the Cannon and Civill lawis.

DILIGENCE.

Father, ȝe man, incontinent,
Passe to the Lords of Parliament ;
For quhy thay ar determinat, all,
2528 To do na thing by ȝour counsall.

You must at
once pass to the
Lords of Parlia-
ment, who will
do nothing
without you.

GVDE-COVNSALL.

That sal I do within schort space ;
Praying the Lord to send vs grace
For till conclude, or wee depart,
2532 That thay may profeit efterwart.
Baith to the Kirk and to the King
I sall desyre na vther thing.

Softly! May we
arrange all,
before we
separate!
Heartily I
desire this.

(*Pausa.*)

My Lords, God glaid the cumpanie !
2536 Quhat is the caus ȝe send for me ?

Why do you
send for me?

MERCHAND.

Sit doun, and gif vs ȝour counsell,
How we sall slaik the greit murmell
Of pure peopill, that is weill knawin,
2540 And as the Common-weill hes schawin.
And, als, wee knaw it is the Kings will,
That gude remeid be put thairtill.
Sir Common-weill, keip ȝe the bar :
2544 Let nane except ȝour self cum nar.

Sit down, and
tell us how the
murmurs of the
poor are to
be stilled.

The King is con-
cerned about this.

Commonwealth,
keep out
intruders.

IOHNE.

That sall I do as I best can :
I sall hauld out baith wyfe and man.
Ȝe man let this puir creature
2548 Support me for till keip the dure.
I knaw his name full sickerly :
He will complaine, als weill as I.

As well as
I am able.

But this
poor creature
must help.

I know him;
and he has com-
plaints to make.

GVDE-COVNSALL.

While busied		My worthy Lords, sen ȝe haue taine on hand
with reform,—	2552	Sum reformatioun to mak into this land,—
seconded by		And als ȝe knaw it is the Kings mynd,
the King,—		Quha till the Common-weil hes, ay, bene kynd,—
you must not		Thocht reif and thift wer stanchit weill aneuch,
only punish robbery.	2556	Ȝit sumthing mair belangis to the pleuch.
In peace you		Now, into peace, ȝe sould provyde for weirs,
should provide		And be sure of how mony thowsand speirs
against war,		The King may be, quhen he hes ocht ado ;
and not as	2560	For quhy, my Lords, this is my ressoun, to :
before, but regular men- at-arms.		The husband-men and commons thay war wont Go, in the battell, formest in the front.
You must be		Bot I haue tint all my experience,
more alert.	2564	Without ȝe mak sum better diligence.
The Common- wealth must be more honoured.		The Common-weill mon vther wayis be styllit ; Or, be my faith ! the King wilbe begyllit.
The Commons		Thir pure commouns, daylie, as ȝe may se,
daily grow poorer.	2568	Declynis doun till extreme povertie ;
Their rents keep		For sum ar hichtit sa into thair maill,
them starved.		Thair winning will nocht find them water-kaill.
Tithes to the		How Prelats heichts thair teinds, it is well
Prelates grieve		knawin,
the husbandmen.	2572	That husband-men may not weill hald thair awin.
Gentle folk,		And now begins ane plague amang them, new,
too, increase		That gentill men thair steadings taks in few :
their grievance.		Thus man thay pay great ferme, or lay thair steid.
They will be ruined, but for God's pity.	2576	And sum ar plainlie harlit out be the heid, And ar distroyit, without God on them rew.

PAVPER.

This is true,		Sir, be Gods breid ! that taill is verie trew.
I had cattle and horses; now, my clothes only.	2580	It is weill kend, I had baith nolt and hors ; Now, all my geir ȝe se vpon my cors.

CORRECTIOVN.

I will mend matters, before I go.	Or I depairt, I think to mak ane ordour.

IOHNE.

I pray ȝow, sir, begin, first, at the bordour,
For how can we fend vs aganis Ingland,

2584 Quhen we can nocht, within our natiue Land,
Destroy our awin Scots common trator theifis,
Quha to leill laborers daylie dois mischeifis?
War I ane King, my Lord, be Gods wounds!

2588 Quhaever held common theifis within thair
bounds,—
Quhairthrow that, dayly, leil men micht be
wrangit,—
Without remeid thair chiftanis suld be hangit.
Quhidder he war ane knicht, ane Lord, or Laird,

2592 The Devill draw me to hell, and he war spaird.

Begin at the border; for how can we defend ourselves against England, if we cannot root out our own thieves? Were I a king, all chieftains that harboured common thieves should be hanged. I would not spare the noblest.

TEMPORALITIE.

Quhat vther enemies hes thou, let vs ken.

What other enemies have you?

IOHNE.

Sir, I compleine vpon the idill men ;
For quhy, sir, it is Gods awin bidding,

2596 All Christian men to wirk for thair living.
Sanct Paull, that pillar of the Kirk,
Sayis to the wretchis that will not wirk,
And bene to vertews laith,

2600 Qui non laborat non manducet,
. This is, in Inglische toung or leit :
Quha labouris nocht he sall not eit.
This bene against the strang beggers,

2604 Fidlers, pypers, and pardoners.
Thir Iugglars, Iestars, and idill cuitchours,
Thir carriers, and thir quintacensours,
Thir babil-beirers, and thir bairds,

2608 Thir sweir swyngeours with Lords and Lairds,
Ma then thair rents may susteine,
Or to thair profeit neidfull bene,

The idle; for all Christians should earn their living. S. Paul says, with reference to such as will not work, and are averse from virtue: ' No labour, no meat.' This, of beggars and the like. Jugglers, jesters, idle gamblers, and people of this sort are a useless expense, and of no sort of profit,

contentious,

Quhilk bene, ay, blythest of discords,

make-baits, 2612 And deidly feid amang thar Lords :

retained for For then they sleutchers man be treatit,

violence. Or els thair querrels vndebaitit.

This is against This bene against thir great fat Freiris,

all that wear 2616 Augustenes, Carmleits, and Cordeleirs,

cowls, who
work not, but And all vthers that in cowls bene cled,

are well fed, Quhilk labours nocht, and bene weill fed :

though every I mein, nocht laborand Spirituallie,

way idle, 2620 Nor, for thair living, corporallie.

like dogs, Lyand in dennis, lyke idill doggis,

or swine. I them compair to weil fed hoggis.

They should I think they do them selfis abuse,

act up 2624 Seing that thay the warld refuse ;

to their Haifing profest sic povertie,

profession. Syne, fleis fast fra necessitie.

What if they Quhat gif thay povertie wald professe,

imitated 2628 And do as did Diogenes,

Diogenes ? That great famous Philosophour ?

Disgusted with Seing, in earth, bot vaine labour,

the world, he
shut himself Alutterlie the warld refusit,

up in a tub, 2632 And in ane tumbe him self inclusit,

and lived on And leifit on herbs and water cauld ;

herbs and water. Of corporall fude na mair he wald.

He did not beg He trottit nocht from toun to toun,

about, but 2636 Beggand to feid his carioun :

freed the world Fra tyme that lyfe he did profes,

of himself. The wald of him was cummerles.

I might instance Rycht sa, of Marie Magdalene,

other cases of 2640 And of Mary th' Egyptiane,

real poverty, And of auld Paull, the first Hermeit,

in hundreds, All thir had povertie compleit.

if I chose. Ane hundreth ma I micht declair ;

In short, slothful 2644 Bot to my purpois I will fair ;

idleness is
injurious to Concluding sleuthfull idilnes

the State. Against the Common-weill expresso.

CORRECTIOVN.

Quhom vpon ma will ȝe compleine ?

Do you complain of any one else ?

IOHNE.

2648 Marie ! on ma, and ma againe.

Of many.

For the pure peopill cryis, with cairis,

The Eyres

The infetching of Iustice airis,

satisfy covet-

Exercit mair for couetice

ousness rathor

2652 Then for the punisching of vyce.

than justice.

Ane peggrell theif that steillis ane kow

A petty thief

Is hangit ; bot he that steillis ane bow,

is hanged ;

With als meikill geir as he may turs,

a wholesale

2656 That theif is hangit be the purs.

robber, fined.

Sic pykand peggrall theifis ar hangit ;

A heinous

Bot he that all the warld hes wrangit,—

transgressor, if

Ane cruell tyrane, ane strang transgressour,

of substance,

2660 Ane common, publick, plaine oppressour,—

will give bribes,

By buds may he obteine fauours

buy favours,

Of Tresurers and compositours :

and, though he

Thocht he serue greit punitioun,

deserves severe

2664 Gets easie compositioun.

punishment, will

get off easily.

And, throch laws consistoriall,

It is no wonder,

Prolixt, corrupt, and perpetuall,

owing to the

The common peopill ar put sa vnder,

consistorial laws,

that the common

2668 Thocht thay be puir it is na wonder.

people are poor

CORRECTIOVN.

Gude Iohne, I grant all that is trew :

It is even so ;

ȝour infortoun full sair I rew.

and I pity you.

Or I pairt aff this Natioun,

But I will reform

2672 I sall mak reformatioun.

all, before I go.

And, als, my Lord Temporalitie,

Lord Tempor-

I ȝow command, in tyme that ȝe

ality, put down

Expell oppressioun aff ȝour lands.

oppression

betimes.

2676 And, als, I say to ȝow, merchands,

Merchants,

if ever I find
you keeping
company with
Deceit, I will
use my sword,
and do strict
justice on you.

Gif ever I find, be land or sie,
Dissait be in ȝour cumpanie,
Quhilk ar to Common-weill contrair,
2680 I vow to God I sall not spair
To put my sword to executioun,
And mak on ȝow extreme punitioun.

Lord Spiritualty,
you are to let
your lands to real
husbandmen, and
not to gentlemen,
that neither will
work nor can.

Mairover, my Lord Spiritualitie,
6684 In gudlie haist I will that ȝe
Set into few ȝour temporall lands
To men that labours with thair hands,
Bot nocht to ane gearking gentill man,
6688 That nether will he wirk, nor can,—
Quhairthroch the policy may incresse.

TEMPORALITIE.

I am willing to do
so, if Spiritualty
does likewise.

I am content, sir,—be the messe !—
Swa that the Spiritualitie
2692 Sets thairs in few, als weill as wee.

CORRECTIOVN.

Spiritual Lords,
are you willing ?

My Spirituall Lords, ar ȝe content ?

SPIRITVALITIE.

We must con-
sider; for it is
not good to re-
solve hastily in
such matters.

Na ! na ! Wee man tak advysement.
In sic maters for to conclude
2696 Ouir haistelie wee think nocht gude.

CORRECTIOVN.

You shall be
punished, if you
do not consent.

Conclude ȝe nocht with the Common-weil,
Ȝe salbe punischit, be Sanct Geill !

(Heir sall the Bischops cum, with the Freir.)

SPIRITVALITIE.

We demur
to your title
to punish us.

Schir, we can schaw exemptioun
2700 Fra ȝour temporall punitioun,
The quhilk wee purpois till debait.

CORRECTIOVN.

Wa! Than ȝe think to stryue for stait !
My Lords, quhat say ȝe to this play ?

So you are
ambitious !

TEMPORALITIE.

2704 My soverane Lords, we will obay,
And tak ȝour part with hart and hand,
Quhatever ȝe pleis vs to command.

We will do
whatever
you command.

(*Heir sal the Temporal stait sit doun on thair knies, & say :*)

Bot wee beseik ȝow, Soveraine,
2708 Of all our cryms that ar bygaine
To gif vs ane remissioun.
And heir wee mak to ȝow conditioun
The Common-weill for till defend
2712 From henceforth till our liues end.

For past crim3s
we crave
forgiveness.

The Common-
wealth we will
ever defend.

CORRECTIOVN.

On that conditioun I am content
Till pardon ȝow, sen ȝe repent.
The Common-weill tak be the hand,
2716 And mak with him perpetuall band.

Then I
pardon you.

Make a league
with the Com-
monwealth.

(*Heir sall the temporal staits, to wit, the Lords and merchands,
imbreasse Iohne the Common-weill.*)

Iohne, haue ȝe ony ma debaits
Against the Lords of Spirituall staits ?

Do you charge
anything further
against the
Spiritual Estate ?

IOHNE.

Na, sir. I dar nocht speik ane word.
2720 To plaint on Preistis, it is na bourd.

I do not dare
to complain
of priests.

CORRECTIOVN.

Flyt on thy fow fill, I desyre the,
Swa that thou schaw bot the veritie.

Blame your
fill, so you
speak truth.

IOHNE.

Grandmerces ! Then I sall nocht spair
2724 First to compleine on the Vickair.

Then, there
is the vicar.

A poor cotter,
who has children,
dies. Of his
two cows the
vicar takes
one, and
the coverlet.

The pure Cottar being lyke to die,
Haifand ȝoung infants, twa or thrie,
And hes twa ky, but ony ma ;
2728 The Vickar most haif ane of thay,
With the gray frugge that covers the bed,
Howbeit the wyfe be purelie cled.

If the wife dies,
he takes
the other cow,
with a coat.

And, gif the wyfe die on the morne,
2732 Thocht all the bairns sould be forlorne,
The vther kow he cleiks away,·
With the pure cot of raploch gray.

Let there be
an end of this.

Wald God this custome war put doun,
2736 Quhilk never was foundit be ressoun !

TEMPORALITIE.

Do you tell
the truth ?

Ar all thay tails trew that thou telles ?

PAVPER.

I recount
my own
experience.

Trew, sir ! The Divill stick me, elles !
For—be the halie Trinitie !—
2740 That same was practeisit on me.

Our vicar
robbed me
of three cows,
for my father,
wife, and mother.

For our Vickar—God giue him pyne !—
Hes ȝit thrie tydie kye of myne ;
Ane for my father, and, for my wyfe, ane vther,
2744 And the thrid cow he tuke for Mald, my mother.

IOHNE.

Our parson takes
his tithes, and
spends them, but
does not preach.

Our Persone, heir, he takis na vther pyne
Bot to ressaue his teinds, and spend them, syne ;
Howbeit he be obleist, be gude ressoun,
2748 To preich the Evangell to his parochoun.

He does not
forego his
comforts.

Howbeit thay suld want preiching sevintin ȝeir,
Our Persoun will not want ane scheif of beir.

PAVPER.

Our bishops
have great wealth,
live in
palaces, and

Our bishops, with thair lustie rokats quhyte,
2752 Thay flow in riches, royallie, and delyte.
Lyke Paradice bene thair palices and places,

And wants na pleasour of the fairest faces.

Als, thir Prelates hes great prerogatyues ;

2756 For quhy thay may depairt, ay, with thair wyues,
Without ony correctioun or damnage,
Syne, tak ane vther wantoner, but mariage.

But doubt, I wald think it ane pleasant lyfe,

2760 Ay on, quhen I list, to part with my wyfe,
Syne, tak ane vther, of far greiter bewtie.

Bot ever, alace ! my Lords, that may not be ;
For I am bund, alace ! in mariage.

2764 Bot thay, lyke rams, rudlie in thair rage,
Vnpysalt, rinnis amang the sillie ʒowis,
Sa lang as kynde of nature in them growis.

have pretty women.

Moreover, they change their wives, and with impunity, scorning wedlock.

I should think this very pleasant.

But I am married.

They indulge their lust as long as it lasts.

PERSON.

Thou lies, fals huirsun, raggit loun.

2768 Thair is na Preists, in all this toun,
That ever vsit sic vicious crafts.

Liar, not a priest in town has ever done thus.

IOHNE.

The feind ressaue thay flattrand chafts !

Sir Domine, I trowit ʒe had be dum.

2772 Quhair Devil gat we this ill-fairde blaitie bum ?

What a simpleton, to say this!

PERSON.

To speik of Preists, be sure it is na bourds.

Thay will burne men, now, ·for rakles words ;

And all thay words ar herisie, in deid.

Such heresy is deserving of the stake.

IOHNE.

2776 The mekil feind resaue the saul that leid !
All that I say is trew, thocht thou be greifit ;
And that I offer on thy pallet to preif it.

I say what is true; and I can prove it.

SPIRITVALITIE.

My lords, quhy do ʒe thoil that lurdun loun

2780 Of Kirk-men to speik sic detractioun ?

Why is t' is varlet allowed to slander the clergy ?

111

This is past joking.

I let ʒow wit, my Lords, it is na bourds
Of Prelats for till speik sic wantoun words.

(Heir Spritualitie fames and rages.)

The villain puts me out of charity.

ʒon villaine puttis me out of Charitie.

TEMPORALITIE.

If he has lied, you have your remedy.

2784   Quhy, my Lord?   Sayis he ocht bot verity?
ʒe can nocht stop ane pure man for till pleinʒe.
Gif he hes faltit, summond him to ʒour Seinʒe.

SPIRITVALITIE.

The wretch shall rue his speaking of the cow.

ʒea, that I sall.   I mak greit God a vow,
2788   He sall repent that he spak of the kow.
I will not suffer sic words of ʒon villaine.

PAVPER.

Then give my three cows back.

Than gar gif me my thrie fat ky againe.

SPIRITVALITIE.

Don't you fear to speak of me?

Fals carle, to speik to me stands thou not aw?

PAVPER.

An hour after my father was dead, the vicar seized my cow.

2792   The feind-resaue them that first devysit that law!
Within an houre efter my dade was deid,
The Vickar had my kow hard be the heid.

PERSON.

That law is good, being of old use.

Fals huirsun carle, I say that law is gude,
2796   Becaus it hes bene lang our consuetude.

PAVPER.

When Pope, I will repeal it.

Quhen I am Paip, that law I sal put doun.
It is ane sair law for the pure commoun.

SPIRITVALITIE.

You shall repent these words.

I mak an vow, thay words thou sal repent.

GVDE-COVNSALL.

2800 I ȝow requyre, my Lords, be patient.
Wee came nocht heir for disputatiouns ;
Wee came to make gude reformatiouns.
Heirfoir, of this ȝour propositioun
2804 Conclude, and put to executioun.

We came,
not to dispute,
but to reform.
Do you take
action, then.

MERCHAND.

My Lords, conclud that al the temporal lands
Be set in few to laboreris with thair hands,
With sic restrictiouns as sall be devysit,
2808 That thay may liue, and nocht to be supprysit,
With ane ressonabill augmentatioun ;
And, quhen thay heir ane proclamatioun,
That the Kings grace dois mak him for the weir,
2812 That thay be reddie with harneis, bow, and speir.
As for myself, my Lord, this I conclude.

Let the temporal
lands be leased
to husbandmen,
on terms which
they can bear.
And let them
hold themselves
in readiness
against being
required for war.

GVDE-COVNSALL.

Sa say we all. Ȝour ressoun be sa gude,
To mak ane Act on this we ar content.

You have only
to make an Act
on this.

IOHNE.

2816 On that, sir Scribe, I tak ane instrument.
Quhat do ȝe of the cors-present and kow ?

What of the
mortuary
and cow ?

GVDE-COVNSALL.

I wil conclude nathing of that, as now,
Without my Lord of Spiritualitie
2820 Thairto consent, with all this haill cleargie.
My Lord Bischop, will ȝe thairto consent ?

What say the
clergy and the
Lord Bishop to
this matter ?

SPIRITVALITIE.

Na, na ! Never till the day of Iudgement
Wee will want nathing that wee haue in vse,—
2824 Kirtil, nor kow. teind lambe, teind gryse, nor
guse.

We will never
give up anything
we have been
used to enjoy.

TEMPORALITIE.

The King had
better apply
to the Pope
for a decree
against mortu-
aries, which
we object to.

Forsuith, my Lord, I think we suld conclude,
Seing this kow ȝe haue in consuetude,
Wee will decerne, heir, that the Kings grace
2828 Sall wryte vnto the Paipis holines.
With his consent, be proclamatioun
Baith cors-present and cow wee sall cry doun.

SPIRITVALITIE.

Record my dis-
sent, notary.

To that, my Lords, wee plainlie disassent.
2832 Noter, thairof I tak ane instrument.

TEMPORALITIE.

It signifies no-
thing that you
object. We two
Estates can carry
it against you one.

My lord, be him that al the warld hes wrocht!
Wee set nocht by quhider ȝe consent or nocht.
ȝe ar bot ane estait, and we ar twa ;
2836 Et vbi maior pars ibi tota.

IOHNE.

Consider, now,
the money that
goes to Rome
in bribes.
If I were a King,
never a penny
more should find
its way there.
There must be a
stop put to this.

My lords, ȝe haif richt prudentlie concludit.
Tak tent, now, how the land is clein denudit
Of gould and silver, quhilk daylie gais to Rome,
2840 For buds, mair then the rest of Christindome.
War I ane King, sir, be coks passioun !
I sould gar mak ane proclamatioun,
That never ane penny sould go to Rome at all,
2844 Na mair then did to Peter nor to Paull.
Do ȝe nocht sa, heir, for conclusioun,
I gif ȝow, all, my braid black malesoun.

MERCHAND.

The complaint
is very just.
We merchants
alone have
sent enormous
wealth thither.

It is of treuth, sirs, be my christindome !
2848 That mekil of our money gais to Rome ;
For we merchants, I wait, within our bounds,
Hes furneist Preists ten hundreth thowsand
        punds,

114

For thair finnance : nane knawis sa weill as wee.

2852 Thairfoir, my Lords, devyse sum remedie ;

For, throw thir playis, and thir promotioun,

Mair for denners nor for devotioun,

Sir Symonie hes maid with them ane band,

2856 The gould of weicht thay leid out of the land ;

The Common-weil thairthroch being sair opprest.

Thairfoir, devyse remeid, as ʒe think best.

Let this be remedied.

So much gold— and not for spiritual pur- poses,—has gone out of the country, that the Commonwealth suffers sorely in consequence.

GVDE-COVNSALL.

It is schort tyme sen ony benefice

2860 Was sped in Rome, except greit Bischopries ;

Bot, now, for ane vnworthie Vickarage

Ane Preist will rin to Rome, in Pilgramage.

Ane cavell quhilk was never at the scule

2864 Will rin to Rome, and keip ane Bischops mule,

And, syne, cum hame, with mony colorit crack,

With ane buirdin of benefices on his back ;

Quhilk bene against the law, ane man alane

2868 For till posses ma benefices nor ane.

Thir greit commends, I say, withoutin faill,

Sould nocht be giuen bot to the blude Royall.

Sa I conclude, my Lords, and sayis, for me,

2872 ʒe sould annull all this pluralitie.

People now visit Rome, not for bishoprics only, but even for vicarships.

A poor illiterate creature will go to Rome, tend a Bishop's mule, and return laden with benefices, in the teeth of the law.

Such abuses, and that of pluralities, should be abolished.

SPIRITVALITIE.

The Paip hes giuen vs dispensatiouns.

The Pope has given us dispensations.

GVDE-COVNSALL.

ʒea, that is, be ʒour fals narratiouns.

Thocht the Paip, for ʒour pleasour, will dispence,

2876 I trow that can nocht cleir ʒour conscience.

Advyse, my Lords, quhat ʒe think to conclude.

You deceiv- ing him. But, even then, you cannot clear your consciences. What shall be done ?

TEMPORALITIE.

Sir, be my faith ! I think it verie gude,

To my mind,

priests should
keep away from
Rome; as they
impoverish the
realm for their
own benefit.

That, fra hencefurth, na Preistis sall pas to
    Rome ;

2880 Becaus our substance thay do still consume.

For pleyis, and for thair profeit singulair,

Thay haif of money maid this realme bair.

And I think a
priest should
have but one
benefice, or none.

And, als, I think it best, be my advyse,

2884 That ilk Preist sall haif bot ane benefice ;

And, gif thay keip nocht that fundatioun,

It sall be caus of deprivatioun.

MERCHAND.

We concur
in this.

As ȝe haif said, my Lord, we wil consent.

2888 Scribe, mak ane act on this, incontinent.

GVDE-COVNSALL.

Now, what is
the duty of
prelates
and priests ?

My Lords, thair is ane thing ȝit vnproponit,—

How Prelats and Preistis aucht to be disponit :

· This beand done, we haue the les ado.

We should decide
this point, before
we break up.

2892 Quhat say ȝe, sirs ? This is my counsall, lo !

That, or wee end this present Parliament,

Of this mater to tak rype advysement.

Benefices are
given for good.

Mark weill, my Lords, thair is na benefice

2896 Giuen to ane man, bot for ane gude office.

An office should
be duly served.

Quha taks office, and syne thay can nocht vs it,

Giuer and taker, I say, ar baith abusit.

A bishop
should preach;

Ane Bischops office is for to be ane preichour,

2900 And of the law of God ane publick teachour ;

and a parson
should teach
the Gospel.

Rycht sa, the Persone vnto his parochoun

Of the Evangell sould leir them ane lessoun.

The clergy ought
to be qualified.

Thair sould na man desyre sic dignities,

2904 Without he be abill for that office ;

Tithes are to
reward services.

And, for that caus, I say, without leising,

They haue thair teinds, and for na vther thing.

SPIRITVALITIE.

Where do you
learn that we
ought to be
preachers ?

Freind, quhair find ȝe that we suld prechours be ?

GVDE-COVNSALL.

2908 Luik quhat Sanct Paul wryts vnto Timothie.   Read what S.
Paul writes
Tak, thair, the Buik : let se gif ȝe can spell.   to Timothy.

SPIRITVALITIE.

I never red that.   Thairfoir, reid it, ȝour sel.   Read it yourself.

(Gude-Counsall sall read thir wordis on ane Buik.)

Fidelis sermo : Si quis Episcopatum desiderat, bonum opus deside-
rat.   Oportet [ergo,] eum irreprehensibilem esse, vnius vxoris
virum, sobrium, prudentem, ornatum, pudicum, hospitalem, The duty
doctorem, non vinolentum, non percussorem, sed modestum.
That is :   of a

This is a true saying : If any man desire the office of a Bishop, Bishop.
he desireth a worthie worke.   A Bishop, therefore, must be vn-
reproueable, the husband of one wife, &c.

SPIRITVALITIE.

ȝe temporall men, be him that heryit hell !   You laymen have
no business with
2912 ȝe ar ovir peart with sik maters to mell.   such things.

TEMPORALITIE.

Sit still, my Lord.   ȝe neid not for til braull.   S. Paul himself
Thir ar the verie words of th' Apostill Paull.   says this.

SPIRITVALITIE.

Sum sayis, be him that woare the croun of Some say it had
thorne !   been well, if
Paul had never
2916 It had bene gude that Paull had neir bene borne. been born.

GVDE-COVNSALL.

Bot ȝe may knaw, my Lord, Sanct Pauls intent. Did you never
read the New
Schir, red ȝe never the New testament ?   Testament ?

SPIRITVALITIE.

Na, sir.   Be him that our Lord Jesus sauld !   Never New
or Old ; nor
2920 I red never the New testament, nor auld ;   do I mean to
Nor ever thinks to do, sir, be the Rude !   read them.
I heir freiris say that reiding dois na gude.   To read is bad.
8

117

GVDE-COVNSALL.

Reading would
be no wrong to
you, it being
your duty.
What do you
say to this ?

2924

Till ȝow to reid them I think it is na lack ;
For, anis I saw them, baith, bund on ȝour
    back,—
That samin day that ȝe was consecrat.
Sir, quhat meinis that ?

SPIRITVALITIE.

Don't pester me.

The feind stick them that wat !

MERCHAND.

You are unfit
for your office.
Your tithes were
never given you
to reward what
you now do.
How very
apostolic !
For tithes
give teachers.

2928

2932

2936

Then befoir God how can ȝe be excusit,
To haif ane office, and waits not how to vs it ?
Quhairfoir war gifin ȝow all the temporal lands,
And all thir teinds ȝe haif amang ȝour hands ?
Thay war giuin ȝow for vther causses, I weine,
Nor mummil matins and hald ȝour clayis cleine.
Ȝe say to the Appostils that ȝe succeid ;
Bot ȝe schaw nocht that into word nor deid.
The law is plaine, our teinds suld furnisch
    teichours.

GVDE-COVNSALL.

Or preachers.

Ȝea, that it sould, or susteine prudent preichours.

PAVPER.

Our parson
never preached.

Sir, God ! nor I be stickit with ane knyfe,
Gif ever our Persoun preichit, in all his lyfe.

PERSONE.

What does our
preaching
concern you ?

2940

Quhat devil raks the of our preiching, vndocht ?

PAVPER.

Should you get
tithes gratis ?

Think ȝe that ȝe suld haue the teinds for nocht ?

PERSONE.

Do you look for
a cure of this ?

Trowis thou to get remeid, carle, of that thing ?

PAVPER.

3ea, be Gods breid ! richt sone, war I ane King. *There would be a cure, if I were king.*

PERSONE.

2944 Wald thou of Prelats mak deprivatioun ? *Would you deprive prelates?*

PAVPER.

Na ; I suld gar them keip thair fundatioun. *Not so.*
Quhat devill is this ?   Quhom of .sould Kings *Why should*
stand aw *kings fear to*
To do the thing that thay sould be the law ? *obey the law?*
2948 War I ane King, be coks deir passioun ! *If there be not*
I sould richt sone mak reformatioun. *a reformation,*
Failƺeand thairof, ƺour grace sould richt sone *the priests will*
finde *soon have it all*
That Preists sall leid ƺow lyke ane bellie blinde. *their own way.*

IOHNE.

2952 Quhat gif King David war leiuand in thir dayis, *If King David,*
The quhilk did found sa mony gay Abayis ! *who founded so many abbeys,*
Or, out of heavin quhat gif he luikit doun, *were now living, or were he to*
And saw the great abominatioun *look down from Heaven and see*
2956 Amang thir Abesses and thir Nunries,— *the corruption of the religious*
Thair publick huirdomes and thair harlotries ! *houses,*
He wald repent he narrowit sa his bounds *he would wish*
Of ƺeirlie rent thriescoir of thowsand pounds. *he had been more liberal.*
2960 His successours maks litill ruisse, I ges, *His successors*
Of his devotioun, or of his holines. *little value his virtues.*

ABBASSE.

How dar thou, carle, presume for to declair, *What imperti-*
Or for to mell the with sa heich a mater ? *nence in you!*
2964 For, in Scotland thair did ƺit never ring,— *Never had we*
I let the wit,—ane mair excellent King. *a better King;*
Of holines he was the verie plant, *and he is, now,*
And now, in heavin, he is ane michtfull Sanct ; *a mighty saint.*

He founded fifteen abbeys,—greatly enriching the church,—unlike present kings.

2968 Becaus that fyftein Abbasies he did found,
Quhairthrow great riches hes ay done abound
Into our Kirk, and daylie ȝit abunds :
Bot kings, now, I trow, few Abbasies founds.

Perdition reward your presumption, in judging so holy a man!

2972 I dar weill say, thou art condempnit in hell,
That dois presume with sic maters to mell.
Fals, huirsun carle, thou art ovir arrogant,
To iudge the deids of sic ane halie Sanct.

IOHNE.

What said James I. of him?

He was too profuse;

and his successors suffered from his holiness.

2976 King Iames the first, Roy of this Regioun,
Said that he was ane sair Sanct to the croun.
I heir men say that he was sumthing blind,
That gaue away mair nor he left behind.

2980 His successours that halines did repent,
Quhilk gart them do great inconvenient.

ABBASSE.

This wretch prates heresy,

and deserves to be burnt,

for speaking against our law and liberty.

My Lord Bishop, I mervel how that ȝe
Suffer this carle for to speik heresie ;

2984 For, be my faith ! my Lord, will ȝe tak tent,
He servis for to be brunt incontinent.
Ȝe can nocht say bot it is heresie,
To speik against our law and libertie.

SPIRITVALITIE.

Let him be charged,

and taken to the stake,

if he merits death.

2988 Sancte pater, I mak ȝow supplicatioun,
Exame ȝon carle ; syne, mak his dilatioun.
I mak ane vow to God omnipotent,
That bystour salbe brunt incontinent.

2992 Venerabill father, I sall do ȝour command :
Gif he seruis deid, I sall sune vnderstand.

(*Pausa.*)

Declare your faith.

Fals, huirsun carle, schaw furth thy faith.

IOHNE.

Me think ʒe speik as ʒe war wraith.

You are angry.

2996 To ʒow I will nathing declair ;
For ʒe ar nocht my ordinair.

It is not to you that I will declare anything.

FLATTRIE.

Quhom in trowis' thou, fals monster mangit ?

Whom do you trust in ?

IOHNE.

I trow to God to se the hangit.

I trust to see you hanged.

3000 War I ane King, be coks passioun !

If I were a king,

I sould gar mak ane congregatioun

I would send

Of all the freirs of the four ordouris,

friars of all

And mak ʒow vagers on the bordours.

sorts packing.

3004 Schir, will ʒe giue me audience,

To Your Ex-

And I sall schaw ʒour excellence—

cellency I

Sa that ʒour grace will giue me leife,—

am willing to

How into God that I beleife.

state my belief.

CORRECTIOVN.

3008 Schaw furth ʒour faith, and feinʒe nocht.

State it, and honestly.

IOHNE.

I beleife in God, that all hes wrocht,

I believe in

And creat everie thing of nocht :

God the Creator;

And in his Son, our Lord Iesu,

and in Christ,

3012 Incarnat of the Virgin trew ;

Virgin-born,

Quha vnder Pilat tholit passioun,

crucified,

And deit for our Salvatioun ;

dead, and

And, on the thrid day, rais againe,

risen again on

3016 As halie scriptour schawis plane.

the third day ;

And, als, my Lord, it is weill kend,

ascended into

How he did to the heavin ascend,

Heaven;

And set him doun at the richt hand

seated at God's

3020 Of God the father, I vnderstand,

right hand;

And sall cum iudge on Dumisday.

who will come to judge at

Quhat will ʒe mair, sir, that I say ?

Doomsday.

CORRECTIOVN.

Say the rest.

Schaw furth the rest. This is na game.

IOHNE.

I believe in
Holy Church,
but not in bishops
or friars,—
a graceless
crew, alto-
gether.

3024   I trow Sanctam Ecclesiam,
      Bot nocht in thir Bischops, nor thir Freirs,
      Quhilk will, for purging of thir neirs,
      Sard vp the ta raw and doun the vther.
3028   The mekill Devill resaue the fidder !

CORRECTIOVN.

John seems a
good Christian.

Say quhat ȝe will, sirs, be Sanct Tan !
Me think Iohne ane gude Christian man.

TEMPORALITIE.

Determine, my
Lords, what shall
be done as
to Prelates.

My Lords, let be ȝour disputatioun.
3032   Conclude, with firm deliberatioun,
      How Prelats, fra thyne, sall be disponit.

MERCHAND.

Benefices should
be given to
preachers only;
and no sheep
to wolves.

Heresy is bred
by bad bishops,
independent of
the prince.

Hence, kings
should give
bishoprics to
such only as
preach through-
out their sees.

And every parson
should preach
in his parish.

I think, for me, evin as ȝe first proponit,
      That the Kings grace sall gif na benefice
3036   Bot till ane peichour that can vse that office.
      The sillie sauls that bene Christis scheip
      Sould nocht be givin to gormand wolfis to keip.
      Quhat bene the caus of all the heresies,
3040   Bot the abusioun of the prelacies ?
      Thay will correct, and will nocht be correctit ;
      Thinkand to na prince thay wil be subiectit :
      Quhairfoir, I can find na better remeid
3044   Bot that thir kings man take it in thair heid,
      That thair be giuen to na man bischopries,
      Except thay preich outthroch thair diosies,
      And ilk persone preich in his parochon :
3048   And this I say, for finall conclusion.

TEMPORALITIE.

Wee think ȝour counsall is verie gude :   We all approve
As ȝe haue said, wee all conclude.   your counsel
Of this conclusioun, Noter, wee mak ane act.   as very good.

SCRYBE.

3052 I wryte all day, bot gets never ane plack.   But my fees ?

PAVPER.

Och ! my Lords, for the halie Trinitie,   Remember the
Remember to reforme the consistorie.   consistory, my
It hes mair neid of reformatioun   Lords, which
                                                 sorely needs
3056 Nor Ploutois court, sir, be coks passioun !   amending.

PERSONE.

Quhat caus hes thou, fals pellour, for to pleinȝe ? Why complain
Quhair was ȝe ever summond to thair seinȝe ?   of the consistory ?

PAVPER.

Marie ! I lent my gossop my mear, to fetch hame I lent my
      coills ;   mare ; and she
3060 And he hir drounit into the querrell hollis.   was drowned.
And I ran to the Consistorie, for to pleinȝe ;   I hastened to the
And thair I happinit amang ane greidie meinȝe.   consistory, to
Thay gaue me, first, ane thing thay call citandum ; lodge a com-
3064 Within aucht dayis, I gat bot lybellandum ;   plaint ; and there
Within ane moneth, I gat ad opponendum ;   I fell among
In half ane ȝeir, I gat interloquendum ;   cunning and
And, syne, I gat—how call ȝe it ?—ad replican-   extortionate
      dum :   lawyers, who
3068 Bot I could never ane word ȝit vnderstand him. had my case
And than thay gart me cast out many plackis,   adjourned and
And gart me pay for four and twentie actis ;   adjourned, and
Bot, or thay came half gait to concludendum,   drained me of all
3072 The feind ane plack was left for to defend him. my money, in
Thus thay postponit me twa ȝeir, with thair traine, payment of
Syne, hodie ad octo, bad me cum againe ;   their fees ;

and they cried
for silver, to the
last; but I never
got my good
mare, after all.
And than thir ruiks thay roupit wonder fast

3076   For sentence silver : thay cryit, at the last.
Of pronunciandum thay maid me wonder faine ;
Bot I gat never my gude gray meir againe.

TEMPORALITIE.

Herein, again, we
will reform.

The law-charges
are excessive.

We will have
it here as it is
in France. The
Spiritualty
shall look after
spiritual matters;
the Temporalty,
after temporal.
My Lords, we mon reforme thir consistory lawis,

3080   Quhais great defame aboue the heavins blawis.
I wist ane man, in persewing ane kow,
Or he had done, he spendit half ane bow.
Sa that the kings honour wee may avance,

3084   Wee will conclude as thay haue done in France.
Let Sprituall maters pas to Spritualitie,
And Temporall maters to Temporalitie :
Quha failȝeis of this sall cost them of thair gude.

3088   Scribe, mak ane act ; for sa wee will conclude.

SPIRITVALITIE.

This goes against
our interest,
which we will
not forego.
That act, my Lords,—plainlie I will declair,—
It is againis our profeit singulair.
Wee will nocht want our profeit, be Sanct Geill !

TEMPORALITIE.

Your interest
is selfish ; and
your consent
does not signify.

Temporal Judges,
not spiritual,
should have
cognizance of
matters temporal.

We have given
our decision.
3092   Ȝour profeit is against the Common-weil.
It salbe done, my Lords, as ȝe haue wrocht :
We cure nocht quhidder ȝe consent, or nocht.
Quhairfoir servis, then, all thir Temporall Iudges,

3096   Gif temporall maters sould seik at ȝow refuges ?
My Lord, ȝe say that ȝe ar Sprituall :
Quhairfoir mell ȝe, than, with things temporall ?
As we haue done conclude, sa sall it stand.

3100   Scribe, put our Acts in ordour, evin fra hand.

SPIRITVALITIE.

To all your Acts
we take exception.
Till all ȝour acts plainlie I disassent.
Notar, thairof I tak ane instrument.

(Heir sall Veritie and Chastitie mak thair plaint at the bar.)

VERITIE.

My Soverane, I beseik ȝour excellence,
3104 Vse Iustice on Spiritualitie,
The quhilk to vs hes done great violence,
Becaus we did rehers the veritie.
Thay put vs close into Captivitie;
3108 And sa remanit into subiectioun,
Into great langour and calamitie,
Till we war fred be King Correctioun.

I beseech that Spiritualty may get his due for his violence to us.

He cast us into bonds, where we lay until released by King Correction.

CHASTITIE.

My lord, I haif great caus for to complaine.
3112 I could get na ludging intill this land,
The Spirituall stait had me sa at disdane. .
With Dame Sensuall thay haue maid sic ane band,
Amang them all na freindschip, sirs, I fand;
3116 And, quhen I came the nobill innis amang,
My lustie Ladie Priores, fra hand,
Out of hir dortour durlie scho me dang.

For my part, I could get no lodging in all the land, owing to the influence of Sensuality.

Even the Lady Prioress drove me out of her dormitory.

VERITIE.

With the advyse, sir, of the Parliament,
3120 Hairtlie we mak ȝow supplicatioun,
Cause King Correctioun tak, incontinent,
Of all this sort examinatioun.
Gif thay be digne of deprivatioun,—
3124 ȝe haue power for to correct sic cases,—
Chease the maist cunning Clerks of this natioun,
And put mair prudent pastours in thair places.
My prudent Lords, I say that pure craftsmen
3128 Abufe sum Prelats ar mair for to commend.
Gar exame them, and sa ȝe sall sune ken
How thay in vertew Bischops dois transcend.

Let King Correction examine all persons of this sort. Let fit clergy be substituted for unfit.

Even poor craftsmen know their business better than some bishops.

SCRIBE.

What is
your craft ?

3132

Thy life and craft mak to thir Kings kend.
Quhat craft hes thow declair that to me plaine.

TAIL3EOVR.

That of tailor,
to make and
to mend.

Ane tail3eour, sir, that can baith mak and mend :
I wait, nane better into Dumbartane.

SCRIBE.

Why called
tailor ?

Quhairfoir of tail3eours beirs thou the styl ?

TAIL3EOUR.

Because I can
make doublets,
coats, and hose.

3136

Becaus, I wait, is nane, within ane myll,
Can better vse that craft, as I suppois ;
For I can mak baith doublit, coat, and hois.

SCRIBE.

And what are
you called ?

How cal thay 3ou, sir, with the schaiping knife ?

SOWTAR.

A shoemaker.

3140

Ane sowtar, sir ; nane better into Fyfe.

SCRIBE.

Why so called?

Tel me quhairfoir ane sowtar 3e ar namit ?

SOWTAR.

Because I make
foot-gear.
I should like to
show a sample
of my skill.

3144

Of that surname I neid nocht be aschamit;
For I can mak schone, brotekins, and buittis.
Gif me the coppie of the Kings cuittis,
And 3e sall se, richt sune, quhat I can do.
Heir is my lasts, and weill wrocht ledder, to.

GVDE-COVNSALL.

Things are,
indeed, out of
order, when very
shoemakers and
tailors surpass,
in their voca-
tions, our
prelates.

3148

3152

O Lord my God   This is an mervelous thing,
How sic misordour in this Realme sould ring.
Sowtars and tail3eours thay ar far mair expert
In thair pure craft, and in thair handie art,
Nor ar our Prelatis in thair vocatioun.
I pray 3ow, sirs, mak reformatioun.

VERITIE.

Alace! alace! Quhat gars thir temporal Kings *Much to blame*
Into the Kirk of Christ admit sic doings? *are kings.*
My Lords, for lufe of Christs passioun, *My Lords, depose*
3156 Of thir ignorants mak depriuatioun, *these ignorant*
Quhilk in the court can do bot flatter and fleich ; *persons, mere flatterers, and*
And put into thair places that can preich. *supersede them.*
Send furth, and seik sum devoit cunning Clarks, *by earnest clerks, that know how*
3160 That can steir vp the peopill to gude warks. *to preach.*

CORRECTIOVN.

As 3e haue done, Madame, I am content. *Diligence, explore*
Hoaw! Diligence, pas hynd, incontinent, *the towns, cities,*
And seik outthrow all towns and cities, *and universities,*
3164 And visie all the vniversities. *and bring hither*
Bring vs sum Doctours of Divinitie, *doctors of*
With licents in the law and Theologie, *divinity, licentiates in law*
With the maist cunning Clarks in all this land. *and theology, and*
3168 Speid sune 3our way, and bring them heir fra *learned clerks,*
hand. *forthwith.*

DILIGENCE.

Quhat gif I find sum halie provinciall, *What if I*
Or minister of the gray freiris all, *find any, besides*
Or ony freir, that can preich prudentlie? *these, that*
3172 Sall I bring them with me in cumpanie? *can preach?*

CORRECTIOVN.

Cair thou nocht quhat estait saever he be, *Let them*
Sa thay can teich and preich the veritie. *be included.*
Maist cunning Clarks with vs is best beluifit : *No matter*
3176 To dignitie thay salbe, first, promuifit. *what their titles,*
Quhidder thay be Munk, Channon, Preist, or *they that can*
Freir, *preach shall*
Sa thay can preich, faill nocht to bring them *be raised, first,*
heir. *to dignity.*

DILIGENCE.

3180

Than fair-weill, sir; for I am at the flicht.
I pray the Lord to send ȝow all gude nicht.

(Heir sall Diligence pas to the palȝeoun.)

TEMPORALITIE.

3184

3188

3192

3196

Sir, we beseik ȝour soverane celsitude
Of our dochtours to haue compassioun,
Quhom wee may na way marie, be the Rude!
Without wee mak sum alienatioun
Of our land, for thair supportatioun;
For quhy the markit raisit bene sa hie,
That Prelats dochtours of this natioun
Ar maryit with sic superfluities,
Thay will nocht spair to gif twa thowsand
            pound,
With thair dochtours, to ane nobill man;
In riches sa thay do superabound.
Bot we may nocht do sa, be Sanct Allane!
Thir proud Prelats our dochters sair may ban,
That thay remaine at hame sa lang vnmaryit.
Schir, let ȝour Barrouns do the best thay can,
Sum of our dochtours, I dreid, salbe miscaryit.

CORRECTIOVN.

3200

My Lord, ȝour complaint is richt ressonabill,
And, richt sa, to our dochtours profitabill.
I think, or I pas aff this natioun,
Of this mater till mak reformatioun.

(Heir sall enter common thift.)

THIFT.

3204

Ga by the gait, man; let me gang.
How Devill came I into this thrang?
With sorrow I may sing my sang,
    And I be taine.

For I haue run baith nicht and day ;   *My legs*
Throw speid of fut I gat away.   *saved me.*
Gif I be kend heir, wallaway !   *If recognized,*
3208   I will be slaine.   *I am lost.*

PAVPER.

Quhat is thy name, man, be thy thrift ?   *What is*
   your name ?

THIFT.

Huirsun, thay call me common thift ;   *Common Theft;*
For quhy I had na vther schift,   *for I live*
3212   Sen I was borne.   *by thieving.*
In Eusdaill was my dwelling place :   *My home was*
Mony ane wyfe gart I cry alace ;   *in Ewisdale,*
At my hand thay gat never grace,   *where I vexed*
3216   Bot ay forlorne.   *the wives.*
Sum sayis, ane king is cum amang vs,   *They say that*
That purposis to head and hang vs.   *a King has come,*
Thair is na grace, gif he may fang vs,   *who means*
3220   Bot on an pin.   *to hang us.*
Ring he, we theifis will get na gude.   *I wish he and all*
I pray God and the halie Rude,   *his kindred had*
He had bene smoird into his cude,   *been smothered in*
3224   And all his kin.   *their chrisoms.*
Get this curst King me in his grippis,   *He would soon*
My craig will wit quhat weyis my hippis.   *do for me.*
The Devill I gif his toung and lippis,   *Let no one delate*
3228   That of me tellis.   *against me.*
Adew ! I dar na langer tarie ;   *Good-bye ! If*
For, be I kend, thay will me carie,   *I am known,*
And put me in ane fierie farie :   *it will fare*
3232   I se nocht ellis.   *ill with me.*
I raife Be him that herryit hell !   *I had almost*
I had almaist forʒet my sell.   *forgot myself.*
Will na gude fallow to me tell   *Will no one*
   tell me where
3236   Quhair I may finde   *I can find*
The Earle of Rothus best haiknay :   *a certain hackney*

I came about,—		That was my earand heir away.
sturdy, and fleet		He is richt starck, as I heir say,
as the wind?	3240	And swift as winde.
Here are my		Heir is my brydill and my spurris,
bridle and spurs.		To gar him lance ovir land and furris.
I should like to		Micht I him get to Ewis durris,
spirit him away.	3244	I tak na cuir.
If I got sight of		Of that hors micht I get ane sicht,
him, we should be		I haife na doubt, ȝit or midnicht,
a long way off		That he and I sould tak the flicht
before midnight.	3248	Throch Dysert mure.
Which is the way		Of cumpanarie, tell me, brother,
to the Stother?		Quhilk is the richt way to the Strother.
My mother would		I wald be welcum to my mother,
like to see me.	3252	Gif I micht speid.
With Lord		I wald gif baith my coat and bonet,
Lindesay's genet,		To get my Lord Lindesayis broun Ionet.
and beyond,		War he beȝond the watter of Annet,
the water		We sould nocht dreid.
of Annand, I		
should not fear.	3256	
What brought		Quhat now, Oppressioun, my maister deir !
you here,		Quhat mekill Devill hes brocht ȝow heir ?
Oppression ?		Maister, tell me the caus, perqueir,
What have		
you done ?	3260	Quhat is that ȝe haue done.

OPPRESSIOVN.

The King		Forsuith, the kings maiestie
set me here.		Hes set me heir, as ȝe may se.
I wish I could		Micht I speik Temporalitie,
see Temporalty.	3264	He wald me releife sone.
Pray stay here		I beseik ȝow, my brother deir,
half an hour.		Bot halfe ane houre for to sit heir.
I was never		Ȝe knaw that I was never sweir
backward to		
defend you.	3268	Ȝow to defend.
Put your leg in		Put in ȝour leg into my place ;
my place.		And heir I sweir, be Gods grace,
I will relieve and		Ȝow to releife within schort space,
release you soon.	3272	Syne, let ȝow wend.

THIFT.

Than, maister deir, gif me ʒour hand,
And mak to me ane faithfull band,
That ʒe sall cum agane fra hand,
3276   Withoutin faill.

Then give me your hand, and promise to return soon certainly.

OPPRESSIOVN.

Tak, thair, my hand, richt faithfullie.
Als, I promit the, verelie,
To gif to the ane cuppill of kye,
3280   In Liddisdaill.

I promise faithfully. And I will give you a couple of cows, too.

(*Thift puts his legs in the stockis.*)

Haif I nocht maid ane honest schift,
That hes betrasit common Thift?
For thair is nocht, vnder the lift,
3284   Ane curster cors.

So I have betrayed Common Theft, the miserable wretch.

I am richt sure that he and I,
Within this hal ʒeir, craftely
Hes stolne ane thowsand scheip and ky,
3288   By meiris and hors.

Within the twelvemonth I am sure he and I have stolen a thousand sheep and kine.

Wald God I war baith sound and haill,
Now liftit into Liddisdaill!
The Mers sould find me beif and kaill.
3292   Quhat rak of bread!

Would I were in Liddisdale! The Mers should feed me well.

War I thair liftit, with my lyfe,
The Devill sould stick me with ane knyfe,
And ever I come againe to Fyfe,
3296   Quhill I war dead.

Once there, I would never more return to Fyfe.

Adew! I leife the Devill amang ʒow:
That in his fingers he may fang ʒow,
With all leill men that dois belang ʒow:
3300   For I may rew
That ever I came into this land;
For quhy, ʒe may weill vnderstand,
I gat na geir to turne my hand.
3304   ʒit anis, adew!

Adieu! The Devil take you and all your loyal men! I regret having ever come here, where my chance has been so poor. Once more, adieu!

(Heir sall Diligence conuoy the thrie Clarks.)

DILIGENCE.

I bring three
clerks, very in-
telligent, able to
preach, and also
to teach Latin. 3308

Sir, I haue brocht vnto ȝour Excellence,
Thir famous Clarks of greit intelligence ;
For to the common peopill thay can preich,
And, in the Scuilis, in Latine toung can teich.

They are a doctor
of divinity and
two licentiates,
altogether godly. 3312

This is ane Doctour of Divinitie ;
And thir twa, Licents, men of gravitie.
I heare men say, thair conversatioun
Is maist in Divine Contemplatioun.

DOCTQVR.

My blessing on
this company.
We come to
serve you,
ready to do
whatever you
command. 3316

Grace, peace, and rest from the hie Trinitie,
Mot rest amang this godlie cumpanie !
Heir ar we cumde, as ȝour obedients,
For to fulfil ȝour iust commandements.
Quhateuir it please ȝour Grace vs to command,
Sir, it sall be obeyit, euin fra hand.

REX HVMANITAS.

Welcome !
Sit down, and
advise us. 3320

Gud freinds, ȝe ar richt welcome to vs all.
Sit doun, all thrie, and geif vs ȝour counsall.

CORRECTIOVN.

Exert yourself
in your office.
First, search out
all that are in-
competent to
fulfil their duties,
and put others in
their places. 3324

You are the head
of this congrega-
tion ; and I will
be diligent to
support you. 3328

Sir, I giue ȝow baith counsal & command,
In ȝour office vse exercitioun ;
First, that ȝe gar search, out throch all ȝour land,
Quha can nocht put to executioun
Thair office efter the institutioun
Of godlie lawis, conforme to thair vocatioun :
Put in thair places men of gude conditioun :
And this ȝe do without dilatioun.
Ȝe ar the head, sir, of this congregatioun,
Preordinat be God omnipotent,
Quhilk hes me send to mak ȝow supportatioun,
Into the quhilk I salbe diligent. 3332

And quhasaever beis inobedient,
And will nocht suffer for to be correctit,
Thay salbe, all, deposit incontinent,
3336 And from ʒour presence they sall be deiectit.

And they who refuse to be corrected shall be deprived.

GVDE-COVNSALL.

Begin, first, at the Spritualitie,
And tak of them examinatioun,
Gif they can vse their divyne dewetie.
3340 And, als, I mak ʒow supplicatioun,
All thay that hes thair offices misvsit,
Of them make haistie depriuatioun,
Sa that the peopill be na mair abusit.

Make a beginning with the Spiritualty; and let all that have misused their offices be forthwith · ejected.

CORRECTIOVN.

3344 ʒe ar ane Prince of Spritualitie.
How haue ʒe vsit ʒour office, now let se.

How have you discharged your duties ?

SPIRITVALITIE.

My Lords, quhen was thair ony Prelats wont
Of thair office till ony King mak count ?
3348 Bot of my office gif ʒe wald haue the feill,
I let ʒow wit, I haue it vsit weill ;
For I tak in my count twyse in the ʒeir,
Wanting nocht, of my teind, ane boll of beir.
3352 I gat gude payment of my Temporall lands,
My buttock-maill, my coattis, and my offrands,
With all that dois perteine my benefice.
Consider, now, my Lord, gif I be wyse.
3356 I dar nocht marie contrair the common law ;
Ane thing thair is, my Lord, that ʒe may knaw.
Howbeit I dar nocht plainlie spouse ane wyfe,
ʒit Concubeins I haue had four or fyfe ;
3360 And to my sons I haue giuin rich rewairds,
And all my dochters maryit vpon lairds.
I let ʒow wit, my Lord, I am na fuill,
For quhy I ryde vpon ane amland Muill.

When did a prelate account to a king ? Still, you shall know all. I look well after creature-comforts, and exact everything that I have a claim to, judiciously. The law forbidding me to marry, I have had four or five concubines. I care for my children, too; and I ride an ambling mule.

9

Also, I
live well.

3364   Thair is na Temporall Lord, in all this land,
        That maks sic cheir, I let ʒow vnderstand.

Further, I
pension divers
temporal lords,
that they may
always take
my part.
And this is all.

        And, als, my Lord, I gif, with gude intentioun,
        To divers Temporall Lords ane ʒeirlie pensioun,
3368   To that intent, that thay, with all thair hart,
        In richt and wrang sal plainlie tak my part.
        Now haue I tauld ʒow, sir, on my best ways,
        How that I haue exercit my office.

                          CORRECTIOVN.

I thought you
should preach
and teach.

3372   I weind ʒour office had bene for til preich,
        And Gods law to the peopill teich.

Why your mitre ?

        Quhairfoir weir ʒe that mytour, ʒe me tell.

                          SPIRITVALITIE.

I don't know.

        I wat nocht, man, be him that herryit hel !

                          CORRECTIOVN,

It means that
you should teach
and preach.

3376   That dois betakin that ʒe, with gude intent,
        Sould teich & preich the auld & New testament.

                          SPIRITVALITIE,

A friar takes my
duties till Easter.

        I haue ane freir to preiche into my place :
        Of my office ʒe heare na mair quhill Pasche.

                          CHASTITIE.

This abbot and
this prioress are
scorners and
hypocrites,

3380   My Lords, this Abbot and this Priores
        Thay scorne thair gods. This is my reason quhy
        Thay beare an habite of feinʒeit halines,
        And, in thair deid, thay do the contrary.

They break
their vows
and live
unchastely.
Examine
into this.

3384   For to liue chaist thay vow solemnitly ;
        Bot, fra that thay be sikker of thair bowis,
        Thay liue in huirdome and in harlotry.
        Examine them, Sir, how thay obserue thair vowis.

                          CORRECTIOVN.

All three shall be
scrutinized.

3388   Sir Scribe, ʒe sall, at Chastities requeist,
        Pas and exame ʒon thrie, in gudlie haist.

SCRIBE

Father Abbot, this counsall bids me speir :
How ʒe haue vsit ʒour Abbay, thay wald heir.
3392 And, als, thir Kings hes giuin to me commissioun
Of ʒour office for to mak inquisitioun.

I am to inquire how you have used your abbey and acquitted yourself of your duties.

ABBOT.

Tuiching my office, I say to ʒow, plainlie,
My Monks and I, we leif richt easelie.
3396 Thair is na Monks, from Carrick to Carraill,
That fairs better, and drinks mair holsum Aill.
My Prior is ane man of great devotioun ;
Thairfoir daylie he gets ane double portioun.

My monks and I lead a jovial life, and eat and drink very satisfactorily.

My prior, a most devout man, gets a double share of ale.

SCRIBE.

3400 My Lords, how haue ʒe keipt ʒour thrie vows ?

How have you kept your three vows ?

ABBAS.

Indeid, richt weill, till I gat hame my bows.
In my Abbay quhen I was sure professour,
Then did I leife as did my predecessour.
3404 My paramours is baith als fat and fair
As ony wench into the toun of Air.
I send my sons to Pareis, to the scullis :
I traist in God that thay salbe na fuillis.
3408 And all my douchters I haue weill providit.
Now iudge ʒe gif my office be weill gydit.

I have lived like my predecessor. My paramours are in capital case; my sons are educated at Paris ; and I provide for my daughters. Don't I do well ?

SCRIBE.

Maister Person, schaw vs gif ʒe can preich.

Parson, can you preach ?

PERSONE.

Thocht I preich not, I can play at the caiche.
3412 I wait thair is nocht ane, amang ʒow all,
Mair ferilie can play at the fut-ball ;
And, for the carts, the tabils, and the dyse,
Aboue all persouns I may beir the pryse.

Though I am not able to preach, I have rare skill in all manner of sports and games.

135

I study my
dress, also.
3416　Our round bonats, we mak them, now, four-
　　　　　nuickit,

Such is my life.
Of richt fyne stuiff, gif ʒow list cum and luik it.

You learn no
more from me.
Of my office I haue declarit to the.

Speir quhat ʒe pleis, ʒe get na mair of me.

SCRIBE.

Now for my
Lady Prioress.

Why did
you turn
Chastity away ?
3420　Quhat say ʒe, now, my Ladie Priores ?

How haue ʒe vsit ʒour office, can ʒe ges ?

Quhat was the caus ʒe refusit harbrie

To this ʒoung lustie Ladie Chastitie ?

PRIORES.

She did not
suit me.

I follow custom ;
and I will en-
lighten you
no further.
3424　I wald haue harborit hir, with gude intent ;

Bot my complexioun thairto wald not assent.

I do my office efter auld vse and wount :

To ʒour Parliament I will mak na mair count.

VERITIE.

Now direct
some of your
cunning
clerks that
can preach,
to make a
sermon out
of hand.
3428　Now caus sum of ʒour cunning Clarks

Quhilk ar expert in heavinlie warks,

And men fulfillit with charitie,

That can weill preiche the veritie,

3432　And gif to sum of them command

Ane sermon for to make fra hand.

CORRECTIOVN.

I will do
so at once.
As ʒe haue said, I am content

To gar sum preich incontinent.

(Pausa.)

You can teach in
the schools, I
know. Now
preach a sermon
in English.
3436　Magister noster, I ken how ʒe can teiche

Into the scuillis, and that richt ornatlie.

I pray ʒow, now, that ʒe wald please to preiche

In Inglisch toung, laud folk to edifie.

DOCTOVR.

I will obey you
straightway,
3440　Soverane, I sall obey ʒow humbillie,

With ane schort sermon, presentlie, in this place,

And schaw the word of God, vnfeinȝeitlie

And sinceirlie, as God will giue me grace.

(Heir sall the Doctour pas to the pulpit, and say :)

: 444 Si vis ad vitam ingredi, serva mandata.

Devoit peopill, Sanct Paull, the preichour, sayis :

The fervent luife and fatherlie pitie

Quhilk God almichtie hes schawin, mony wayis,

;448 To man, in his corrupt fragilitie,

Exceids all luife in earth, sa far that we

May never to God mak recompence conding ;

As quhasa lists to reid the veritie

3452 In halie Scripture, he may find this thing.

Sic Deus dilexit mundum.

Tuiching nathing the great prerogatiue

Quhilk God to man, in his creatioun, lent.—

3456 How man, of nocht creat, superlatiue

Was to the Image of God omnipotent,—

Let vs consider that speciall luife ingent,

God had to man, quhen our foirfather fell,

3460 Drawing vs, all, in his loynis immanent,

Captive from gloir, in thirlage to the hel.

Quhen Angels fell, thair miserabil ruyne

Was never restorit ; bot, for our miserie,

3464 The Son of God, secund persone divyne,

In ane pure Virgin tuke humanitie.

Syne, for our saik, great harmis suffered he,

In fasting, walking, in preiching, cauld, and heit ;

3468 And, at the last, ane schamefull death deit he ;

Betwix twa theifis, on Croce, he ȝeild the Spreit :

And, quhair an drop of his maist precious blude

Was recompence sufficient and conding

3472 Ane thowsand warlds to ransoun from that wod

Infernall feind, Sathan, notwithstanding,

He luifit vs sa, that, for our ransoning,

He sched furth all the blude of his bodie,—

3476 Riven, rent, and sair wondit, quhair he did hing,

(marginal notes)
as God shall give me grace.

Devout people, S. Paul teaches us that God's good-will to fallen and frail man surpasses all earthly love, and that we can make no meet return for it.

And this you will find in the Scriptures.

I shall not now dwell on the fact, that God created man in His own image.

Rather, let us consider God's great love to man, when Adam fell, and we with him.

Angels fell, to remain fallen ; but Christ assumed humanity, to rescue man.

Sorely did He suffer for us, and, at last, was crucified, between two thieves.

A single drop of His blood would suffice to redeem a thousand worlds ; and yet, for love of us, He shed all His blood,

137

oh the cross
oñ Calvary.
Naild on the Croce, on the Mont Calvary.

Et copiosa apud eum redemptio.

Thus was
O cruell death, be the the venemous

Satan worsted,
3480 Dragon, the Devill infernall, lost his pray.

we were saved
Be the the stinkand, mirk, contageous,

from hell,
Deip pit of hell mankynd escaipit fray.

and the gate
Be the the port of Paradice, alsway,

of Paradise
3484 Was patent maid vnto the heavin sa hie,—

was opened to
Opinnit to man and maid ane reddie way

all mankind.
To gloir eternall with th' haly Trinitie.

For this love
And ȝit, for all this luife·incomparabill,

God asks
3488 God askis na rewaird fra vs againe,

only love.
Bot luife for luife. In his command, but fabill,

And love is a
Conteinit ar all haill the lawis ten,

ladder with
Baith ald and new, and commandements ilk ane.

but two steps,
3492 Luife bene the ledder, quhilk hes bot steppis twa,

by which we
Be quhilk we may clim vp to lyfe againe,

guin Heaven.
Out of this vaill of miserie and wa.

Diliges Dominum Deum tuum ex toto corde
tuo, & proximum tuum sicut teipsum :
in his duobus mandatis, &c.

First, love
God ; and,
secondly,
love your
neighbour.
3496 The first step, suithlie, of this ledder is,

To luife thy God, as the fontaine and well

Of luife and grace ; and the secund, I wis,

To luife thy nichtbour as thou luifis thy sell.

Otherwise,
there is no
salvation.
So says the
holy Gospel.
3500 Quha tynis ane stop of thir twa, gais to hel,

Bot he repent, and turne to Christ anone.

Hauld this na fabill : the halie Evangell

Bears, in effect, thir words, everie one.

3504 Si vis ad vitam ingredi, serva mandata Dei.

There is
no remedy
for such as
do.not eschew
all manner
of sin, and engage
in good works.
Thay tyne thir steps, all thay quha ever did sin

In pryde, invy, in ire, and lecherie,

In covetice, or ony extreme win,

3508 Into sweirnes, or into gluttonie ;

Or quha dois nocht the deids of mercie,

Gif hungrie meit, and gif the naikit clayis.

PERSONE.

Now, walloway! Thinks thou na schame to lie? *This is*
3512 I trow, the Devill a word is trew thou sayis. *all false.*
Thou sayis thair is bot twa steppis to the heavin; *It is not two*
Quha failȝeis them man backwarts fall in hell. *steps to Heaven,*
I wait it is ten thowsand mylis and sevin: *but many*
3516 Gif it be na mair, I do it vpon thy sell. *thousand miles.*
Schort-leggit men, I se, be Bryds bell! *Short-legged men*
Will nevir cum thair, thay steppis bene sa wyde. *will never get there.*
Gif thay be the words of the Evangell, *One must*
3520 The sprituall men hes mister of ane gyde. *have a guide.*

ABBOT.

And I beleif that cruikit men and blinde *How about the*
Sall neuer get vp vpon sa hich ane ledder. *lame and blind?*
By my gude faith, I dreid to ly behinde, *I must be*
3524 Without God draw me vp into ane tedder. *hauled up.*
Quhat and I fal? Than I will break my bledder. *And if I fall?*
And I cum thair this day, the Devill speid me, *To get up, God*
Except God make me lichter nor ane fedder, *must make me lighter than a*
3528 Or send me doun gude Widcok wingis to flie. *feather, or give me good wood-cocks' wings.*

PERSONE.

Cum doun, dastart, and gang sell draiff. *Come down,*
I vnderstand nocht quhat thow said. *dastard, and go*
Thy words war nather corne nor caiff: *your way. You*
3532 I wald thy toung againe war laid. *prate nonsense.*
Quhair thou sayis pryde is deidlie sin, *Pride is*
I say pryde is bot honestie; *honesty;*
And Covetice of warldlie win *covetousness is*
3536 Is bot wisdome, I say for me: *wisdom;*
Ire, hardines, and gluttonie *and anger and*
Is nathing ellis but lyfis fude: *the rest, which*
The naturall sin of lecherie *you denounce,*
3540 Is bot trew luife. All thir ar gude. *are, all, good.*

DOCTOVR.

God and the Kirk hes giuin command
That all gude Christian men refuse them.

PERSONE.

Bot, war thay sin, I vnderstand,
3544 We men of Kirk wald never vse them.

DOCTOVR.

Brother, I pray the Trinitie
3our faith and charitie to support,
Causand 3ow knaw the veritie,
3548 That 3e 3our subiects may comfort.
To 3our prayers, peopill, I recommend
The rewlars of this nobill regioun ;
That our Lord God his grace mot to them send,
3552 On trespassours to mak punitioun.
Prayand to God from feinds 3ow defend,
And of 3our sins to gif 3ow full remissioun,
I say na mair : to God I 3ow commend.

(*Heir Diligence spyis the freir roundand to the Prelate.*)

DILIGENCE.

3556 My lords, I persaue that the Sprituall stait,
Be way of deid, purpois to mak debait ;
For, be the counsall of 3on flattrand freir,
Thay purpois to mak all this toun on steir.

FIRST LICENT.

3560 Traist 3e that thay wilbe inobedient
To that quhilk is decreitit in Parliament ?

DILIGENCE.

Thay se the Paip, with awfull ordinance,
Makis weir against the michtie King of France.
3564 Richt sa, thay think that prelats suld nocht sun3ie,
Be way of deid, defend thair patrimonie.

FIRST LICENT.

I pray the, brother, gar me vnderstand
Quhair ever Christ possessit ane fut of land.

Where did Christ possess land ?

DILIGENCE.

3568 3ea, that he did, father, withoutin fail ;
For Christ Iesus was King of Israell.

He had land; for He was King of Israel.

FIRST LICENT.

I grant that Christ was king abufe al kings ;
Bot he mellit never with temporall things ;
3572 As he hes plainlie done declair, him sell ;
As thou may reid in his halie Evangell :
Birds hes thair nests, and tods hes thair den ;
Bot Christ Iesus, the Saviour of men,
3576 In all this warld hes nocht ane penny braid
Quhairon he may repois his heavinlie head.

Christ was, indeed, King of kings; but He avoided temporal matters.

Thus, we read, in the Gospel, that He had not where to lay His head.

DILIGENCE.

And is that trew ?

And is this true ?

[SECVND LICENT.]

3es, brother, be Alhallows !
3580 Christ Iesus had na propertie bot the gallows,
And left not, quhen he 3eildit vp the Spreit,
To by himself ane simpill winding-scheit.

It is. He had no property but the Cross; and He did not leave enough to buy a winding-sheet.

DILIGENCE.

Christs successours, I vnderstand,
3584 Thinks na schame to haue temporall land.
Father, they haue na will, I 3ow assure,
In this warld to be indigent and pure.
Bot, sir, sen 3e ar callit sapient,
3588 Declair to me the caus, with trew intent,
Quhy that my lustie Ladie Veritie
Hes nocht bene weill treatit in this cuntrie.

His successors scorn not wealth, unwilling to be poor.

But why was not Lady Truth treated well in this country ?

BATCHELER.

Where the
counsels of
begging friars
prevail, un-
doubtedly the
truth is despised,
causing confusion.

Forsuith, quhair Prelats vses the counsall
3592   Of beggand freirs, in monie regioun,
And thay Prelats, with Princes principall,
The veritie, but doubt, is trampit doun,
And Common-weill put to confusioun.

Is not it so?
3596   Gif this be trew, to ȝow I me report.

Institute
Thairfoir, my Lords, mak reformatioun,

a reform.
Or ȝe depart, hairtlie I ȝow exhort.

Friars prefer to do
Sirs, freirs wald never, I ȝow assure,

the preaching.
3600   That ony Prelats vsit preiching :

They would
lose, if the
prelates did it.
And Prelats tuke on them that cure,
Freirs wald get nathing for thair fleiching.

So banish that
Thairfoir, I counsall ȝow, fra hand

friar, at once,
3604   Banische ȝon freir out of this land,

from the land.
And that incontinent.

Otherwise,
Do ȝe nocht sa, withoutin weir

he will surely
He will mak all this toun on steir :

work mischief.
3608   I knaw his fals intent.

And the prioress
Ȝon Priores, withoutin fabill,

is of evil
I think scho is nocht profitabill

influence.
For Christis regioun.

You should
3612   To begin reformatioun,

deprive them
Mak of them deprivatioun :

both, I think.
This is my opinioun.

FIRST SERGEANT.

If ordered,
Sir, pleis ȝe that we twa invaid them,

we will soon
3616   And ȝe sall se vs sone degraid them

despoil them.
Of coill and chaplarie.

CORRECTIOVN.

Let them be
Pas on.   I am richt weill content.

banished the
Syne, banische them, incontinent,

country directly.
3620   Out of this cuntrie.

FIRST SERGEANT.

Come, friar.
The King must
be obeyed;
Cum on, sir freir, and be nocht fleyit.
The King, our maister, mon be obeyit ;

Bot ȝe sall haue na harme.
3624 Gif ȝe wald travell fra toun to toun,
I think this hude and heauie goun
Will hald ȝour wambe ovir warme.

but you shall take no harm. If you would travel, this hood and gown will keep you warm.

FLATTERIE FREIR.

Now, quhat is this that thir monsters meins?
3628 I am exemptit fra Kings and Queens,
And fra all humane law.

What mean these monsters ? I am not subject to human laws.

SECVND SERGEANT.

Tak ȝe the hude, and I, the gown.
This limmer luiks als lyke ane lown
3632 As any that ever I saw.

Let us take the hood and gown. How like a scamp he looks !

FIRST SERGEANT.

Thir freirs, to chaip punitioun,
Haulds them at their exemptioun,
And na man will obey.
3636 Thay ar exempt, I ȝow assure,
Baith fra Paip, kyng, and Empreour;
And that maks all the pley.

These friars, to escape punish- ment, claim exemption. They are altogether ex- empt, I assure you.

SECVND SERGEANT.

On Dumisday, quhen Christ sall say
3640 Venite benedicti,
The Freirs will say, without delay,
Nos sumus exempti.

At the Judgment, when Christ shall say ' Come, ye blessed,' the friars will say they are exempt.

(*Heir sall thay spuilȝe Flattrie of the Freirs habite.*)

GVDE-COVNSALL.

Sir, be the halie Trinitie !
3644 This same is feinȝeit Flattrie :
I ken him be his face.
Beleiuand for to get promotioun,
He said that his name was Devotioun,
3648 And sa begylit ȝour grace.

I see this is Flattery, in disguise. To get promotion, he called himself Devotion, and so decieved you.

FIRST SERGEANT.

Come on, Lady
Prioress. We
will teach you
a new dance.

Cum on, my Ladie Priores.
   We sall leir ȝow to dance—
And that within ane lytill space,—
3652   Ane new pavin of France.

*(Heir sall thay spuilȝe the Priores ; and scho sall haue ane
kirtill of silk vnder hir habite.)*

Methinks this
holy prioress
has turned into
a courtesan.

Now, brother, be the Masse !
   Be my iudgement, I think
This halie Priores
3656   Is turnit in ane cowclink.

PRIORES.

Curse on my
friends, who
would have me
a nun, and
not marry !

I gif my freinds my malisoun,
   That me compellit to be ane Nun,
     And wald nocht let me marie.

It was their
greed that made
me a prioress.

3660   It was my freinds greadines
   That gart me be ane Priores :
     Now hartlie them I warie.

Nuns sing ever,
but with no
understanding.

Howbeit that Nunnis sing nichts and dayis,
3664   Thair hart waitis nocht quhat thair mouth sayis ;
     The suith I ȝow declair.

They are not
necessary to
the Church.

Makand ȝow intimatioun,
   To Christis congregatioun
3668   Nunnis ar nocht necessair.

I mean to marry,
and become
housewife.

Bot I sall do the best I can,
   And marie sum gude honest man,
     And brew gude aill and tun.

Marriage is more
religious than to
be friar or nun.

3672   Mariage, be my opinioun,
   It is better Religioun
     As to be freir or Nun.

FLATTERIE FREIR.

My Lords, don't
let me be hanged.
I cannot

My Lords, for Gods saik let not hang me,
3676   Howbeit that widdiefows wald wrang me.
     I can mak na debait

To win my meat at pleuch nor harrowis ;
Bot I sall help to hang my marrowis,—

3680   Baith Falset and Dissait.

earn my bread by tillage ; but I can help to hang my companions.

CORRECTIOVN.

Than pas thy way, & greath the gallous ;
Syne, help for to hang vp thy fellowis.
    Thou gets na vther grace.

Then go and prepare the gallows for them. You get no grace but this.

[FLATTERIE.]

3684 Of that office I am content.
Bot our Prelates, I dread, repent,
    Be I fleimde from thair face.

I consent. But our prelates will miss me.

(*Heir sall Flattrie sit besyde his marrowis.*)

DISSAIT.

Now, Flattrie, my auld compan3eoun,
3688 Quhat dois 3on King Correctioun ?
    Knawis thou nocht his intent ?
Declair to vs of thy novellis.

What is Correction doing ? Tell me what you know.

[FLATTERIE.]

3e'ill all be hangit,—I se nocht ellis,—
3692   And that incontinent.

I only know that you will all be hanged.

DISSAIT.

Now, walloway ! Will 3e gar hang vs ?
The Devill brocht 3on curst king amang vs,
    For mekill sturt and stryfe.

Through you ? It was the Devil that brought Correction here.

FLATTERIE.

3696 I had bene put to deid amang 3ow,
War nocht I tuke on hand till hang 3ow ;
    And sa I saifit my lyfe.
I heir them say, thay will cry doun
3700 All freirs and Nunnis in this Regioun,
    Sa far as I can feill,

To save myself, I offered to hang you. All friars and nuns are to be cried down, as unnecessary,

and as opposed
to the common
welfare.

Becaus thay ar nocht necessair :

And, als, thay think thay ar contrair

3704   To Iohne the common-weill.

(Heir sal the Kings and the temporal stait round togider.)

CORRECTIOVN.

These prelates

shall, all,

be deprived;

and these three

clerks shall

supersede them.

This is because
God's Word
was neglected.

With the advice of King Humanitie,

Heir I determine, with rype advysement,

That all thir Prelats sall deprivit be,

3708   And, be decreit of this present Parliament,

That thir thrie cunning Clarks sapient

Immediatlie thair places sall posses ;

Becaus that thay haue bene sa negligent,

3712   Suffring the word of God for till decres.

REX HVMANITAS.

Be it so.

Effect the change.

As ȝe haue said, but dout it salbe done,

Pas to, and mak this interchainging sone,

(The Kings servants lay hands on the thrie prelats, & says :)

WANTONNES.

Patience !

We will obey.

My Lords, we pray ȝow to be patient ;

3716   For we will do the Kings commandement,

SPIRITVALITIE.

Touch us, and

we curse you ;

and, afterwards,
we will complain
to the Pope.

Such reformation

is new in Scotland.

I mak ane vow to God, and ȝe vs handill,

Ȝe salbe curst and gragit with buik and candill.

Syne, we sall pas vnto the Paip, and pleinȝie,

3720   And to the Devill of hell condemne this meinȝe ;

For quhy sic reformatioun, as I weine,

Into Scotland was never hard nor seine.

*(Heir sal thay spuilȝe them with silence, and put thair habite on
the thrie Clarks.)*

MERCHAND.

How could
you accept
such cures,—

We mervell of ȝow, paintit sepulturis,

3724   That was sa bauld for to accept sic cuiris,—

146

With glorious habite rydand vpon ȝour Muillis.   *fools, as you*
Now men may se, ȝe ar bot verie fuillis.   *now appear!*

SPIRITVALITIE.

We say, the Kings war greiter fuillis nor we,   *The kings that*
3728   That vs promovit to sa greit dignitie,   *exalted us were greater fools.*

ABBOT.

Thair is ane thowsand in the kirk, but doubt,   *The Church has*
Sic fuillis as we, gif thay war weill socht out.   *many more like us.*
Now, brother, sen it may na better be,   *But let us go*
3732   Let vs ga soup with Sensualitie.   *drink with Sensuality.*

(*Heir sall thay pas to Sensualitie.*)

SPIRITVALITIE.

Madame, I pray ȝow mak vs thrie gude cheir.   *Madame, pray*
We cure nocht to remaine with ȝow all ȝeir.   *treat us.*

SENSVALITIE.

Pas fra vs, fuillis, be him that hes vs wrocht!   *Away! I will*
3736   Ȝe ludge nocht heir; becaus I knaw ȝow nocht.   *have nothing to do with you.*

SPIRITVALITIE.

Sir Covetice, will ȝe, also, misken me?   *You will help us,*
I wait, richt weill, ȝe wil baith gif and len me.   *Covetousness?*
Speid hand, my freind; spair nocht to break the   *Break open my*
    lockis: *box, and give me a thou-*
3740   Gif me ane thowsand crouns out of my box.   *sand crowns.*

COVETICE.

Quhairfoir, sir fuil, gif ȝow ane thowsand crowns?   *Why give them to*
Ga hence.   Ȝe seime to be thrie verie lowns.   *you? Be off!*

SPIRITVALITIE.

I se nocht els, brother, withoutin faill,   *The world is*
3744   Bot this fals warld is turnit top ouir taill.   *turned topsy-turvy.*
Sen all is vaine that is vnder the lift,   *We must seek a*
To win our meat we man mak vther schift.   *living otherwise.*

<table>
<tr><td>If we do not work, we shall starve.</td><td>3748</td><td>With our labour except we mak debait, I dreid, full sair, we want baith drink and meat.</td></tr>
</table>

If we do not
work, we
shall starve.   3748   With our labour except we mak debait,
I dreid, full sair, we want baith drink and meat.

PERSONE.

Then let us go
where we are
not known.   Gif with our labour we man vs defend,
Then let vs gang quhair we war never kend.

SPIRITVALITIE.

It is these friars
that have ruined   3752   I wyte thir freirs, that I am thus abusit;
me, by usurp-   For by thair counsall I haue bene confusit.
ing my place   Thay gart me trow it suffysit, allace!
in preaching.   To gar them plainlie preich into my place.

ABBOT.

Curse on this
reformation! For   Allace! This reformatioun I may warie;
I have, still, two   3756   For I haue ȝit twa dochters for to marie;
daughters to   And thay ar baith contractit, be the Rude!
marry, and lack
portions for them.   And waits nocht how to pay thair tocher-gude.

PERSONE.

As for me, being   The Devill mak cair for this vnhappie chance ;.
young, I will   3760   For I am ȝoung, and thinks to pas to France,
go to France, and   And tak wages amang the men of weir,
turn soldier.   And win my living with my sword and speir.

(The Bischop, Abbot, persone, and Priores departs, altogidder.)

GVDE-COVNSALL.

Before you go,
let John the   Or ȝe depairt, sir, aff this Regioun,
Commonwealth   3764   Gif Iohne the common-weill ane gay garmoun.
be dressed out;   Becaus the Common-weill hes bene overluikit,
for he has been
neglected,   That is the caus that Common-weill is cruikit.

and is in   With singular profeit, he hes bene sa supprysit,
much distress.   3768   That he is baith cauld, nakit, and disgysit.

CORRECTIOVN.

Be it so.
Deck him   As ȝe haue said, father, I am content.
bravely; and   Sergeants, gif Iohne ane new abuilȝement,—

148

Of Sating, Damais, or of the Velvoit fyne ;—
3772 And gif him place in our Parliament, syne.

(Heir sal thay cleith Iohne the Common-weil gorgeouslie, and set him doun amang them, in the Parliament.)

All verteous peopil now may be reioisit,
Sen Common-weill hes gottin ane gay garmoun ;
And, ignorants out of the Kirk deposit,
3776 Devoit Doctours and Clarks of renoun
Now, in the Kirk, sall haue dominioun ;
And Gude-counsall, with Ladie Veritie,
Ar profest with our kings Maiestie.

3780 Blist is that Realme that hes ane prudent King,
Quhilk dois delyte to heir the veritie,
Punisching thame that plainlie dois maling
Contrair the Common-weill and equitie.

3784 Thair may na peopill haue prosperitie,
Quhair ignorance hes the dominioun,
And common-weil be tirants trampit doun.

(Pausa.)

Now, maisters, ʒe sall heir, incontinent,
3788 At great leysour, in ʒour presence, proclamit
The Nobill Acts of our Parliament,
Of quhilks we neid nocht for to be aschamit.

Cum heir, trumpet, & sound ʒour warning tone,
3792 That every man may knaw quhat we haue done.

(Heir sall Diligence, with the Scribe and the trumpet, pas to the pulpit, and proclame the Actis.)

THE FIRST ACT.

IT is devysit be thir prudent Kings,
Correctioun and King Humanitie,
That thair Leigis, induring all thair Ringis,
3796 With the avyce of the estaits thrie,
Sall manfullie defend and fortifie
The Kirk of Christ, and his Religioun,

10

give him a
seat in our
Parliament.

Rejoice, now,
good people : for
the Common-
wealth has got a
gay garment ;
ignoramuses, in
the Church, have
been exchanged
for fit clerics;
and Good Counsel
and Truth are
friends with
the King.
Happy is the
realm whose
king loves
truth and
punishes in-
justice.

There is no
prosperity
under ignorance
and tyranny.

You shall now
hear the Acts
of our Parliament
proclaimed.
Summon all,
to hear what
we have done.

King Correct-
ion and King
Humanity
have resolved
that their
lieges shall
defend the
Church, and

earnestly, under pain of punishment.	Without dissimulance or hypocrisie,
	3800 Vnder the paine of thair punitioun.
The Acts passed by the last Parliament, being wholesome,	2. Als, thay will, that the Acts honorabill
	Maid, be our Prince, in the last Parliament,
	Becaus thay ar baith gude and profitabill,—
shall be	3804 Thay will that everie man be diligent
duly observed;	Them till observe, with vnfeinʒeit intent.
and they that	Quha disobeyis, inobedientlie,
break them	Be thir lawis, but doubt, thay sall repent,
shall suffer.	3808 And painis conteinit thairin sall vnderly.
The temporal lands are to be leased, as in France,	3. And, als, the Common-weil for til advance,
	It is statute that all the Temporall lands
	Be set in few, efter the forme of France,
	3812 Til verteous men that labours with thair hands,
to real husband- men, but with equitable restrictions.	Resonabillie restrictit with sic bands,
	That thay do service, nevertheles,
	And to be subiect, ay, vnder the wands ;
	3816 That riches may with policie incres.
Noblemen are not to connive at thieves, but are to be re- sponsible for their stealing, if they do not commit them for trial.	4. Item, this prudent Parliament hes devysit,
	Gif Lords halds vnder thair dominioun
	Theifis, quhairthroch puir peopil bein sup- prisit,
	3820 For them thay sall make answeir to the croun,
	And to the pure mak restitutioun,
	Without thay put them in the iudges hands,
	For thair default to suffer punitioun ;
	3824 Sa that na theifis remaine within thair lands.
Justices, with a President, are to be appointed in Elgin, or in Inverness, for the northern quarters, to save long journeys.	5. To that intent, that Iustice sould incres,
	It is concludit, in this Parliament,
	That, into Elgin, or into Inuernesse,
	3828 Sall be ane sute of Clarks sapient,
	Togidder with ane prudent Precident,
	To do iustice in all the Norther Airtis,
	Sa equallie, without impediment,
	3832 That thay neid nocht seik iustice in thir pairts.

6. With licence of the Kirks halines,
That iustice may be done continuallie,
All the maters of Scotland, mair and les,
3836   To thir twa famous saits, perpetuallie,
Salbe directit ; becaus men seis, plainlie,
Thir wantoun Nunnis ar na way necessair
Till Common-weill, nor ʒit to the glorie
3840   Of Christs Kirk, thocht thay be fat and fair.
And, als, that fragill ordour feminine
Will nocht be missit in Christs Religioun :
Thair rents vsit till ane better fyne,
3844   For Common-weill of all this Regioun.
Ilk Senature, for that erectioun,
For the vphalding of thair gravitie,
  · Sall haue fyue hundreth mark of pensioun ;
3848   And, also, bot twa sall thair nummer be.
Into the North, saxteine sall thair remaine ;
Saxtein, rycht sa, in our maist famous toun
Of Edinburgh, to serue our Soveraine ;
3852   Chosen, without partiall affectioun,
Of the maist cunning Clarks of this Regioun ;
Thair Chancellar chosen of ane famous Clark,
Ane cunning man of great perfectioun,
3856   And, for his pensioun, haue ane thowsand mark.
7. It is devysit, in this Parliament,
From this day furth, na mater Temporall—
Our new Prelats thairto hes done consent,—
3860   Cum befoir Iudges consistoriall,
Quhilk hes bene sa prolixt and partiall,
To the great hurt of the communitie.
Let Temporall men seik Iudges Temporall ;
3864   And Sprituall men, to Spritualitie.
8. Na benefice beis giffin, in tyme cumming,
Bot to men of gude eruditioun,
Expert in the halie Scripture, and cunning,
3868   And that they be of gude conditioun,

The Church assenting, spiritual matters are there to be adjudicated on.

Nuns, as being unnecessary either to State or Church, are to be abolished ; and their revenues are to be applied more for the public interest.

The Senators are to be stipendiary, and their number is to be fixed.

There are to be thirty-two royal councillors, chosen, impartially, for their ability ;

and their Chancellor, a learned man, is to have 1000 marks, as salary.

From this day forth, temporal matters shall come before temporal judges, and spiritual matters before spiritual judges.

Benefices are to be bestowed on erudite ecclesiastics,

Of publick vices but supitioun,

And qualefiet richt prudentlie to preich

To thair awin folk, baith into land and toun,

3872 Or ellis in famous scullis for to teich.

[9.] Als, becaus of the great pluralitie

Of ignorant Preists, ma then ane Legioun,—

Quhairthroch of Teicheouris the heich dignitie

3876 Is vilipendit in ilk Regioun,—

Thairfoir our Court hes maid ane provisioun,

That na Bischops mak teichours, in tyme cum-
    ming,

Except men of gude eruditioun,

3880 And for Preistheid qualefeit and cunning.

Siclyke as ʒe se, in the borrows toun,

Ane Tailʒeour is nocht sufferit to remaine,

Without he can mak doublet, coat, and gown,—

3884 He man gang till his prentischip againe,—

Bischops sould nocht ressaue, me think certaine,

Into the Kirk except ane cunning Clark.

Ane ideot preist Esay compaireth, plaine,

3888 Till ane dum dogge, that can nocht byte nor bark.

10. From this day furth, se na Prelats pretend,

Vnder the paine of inobedience,

At Prince or Paip to purchase ane command

3892 Againe the kow; becaus it dois offence.

Till ony Preist we think sufficience

Ane benefice for to serue God withall.

Twa Prelacies sall na man haue, from thence,

3896 Without that he be of the blude Royall.

11. Item, this prudent counsall hes concludit,

Sa that our haly Vickars be nocht wraith,

From this day furth, thay salbe cleane denudit

3900 Baith of cors-present, cow, and vmest claith;

To pure commons becaus it hath done skaith.

And, mairouer, we think it lytill force,

Howbeit the Barrouns thairto will be laith,

3904 From thine furth thay sall want thair hyrald
     hors.

    12. It is decreit, that, in this Parliament,
Ilk Bischop, Minister, Priour, and Persoun,
To the effect thay may tak better tent
3908 To saulis vnder thair dominioun,
Efter the forme of thair fundatioun,
Ilk Bischop in his Diosie sall remaine,
And everilk Persone in his parachoun,
3912 Teiching thair folk from vices to refraine.

    13. Becaus that clarks our substance dois
    consume
For bils and proces of thair prelacies,
Thairfoir thair sall na money ga to Rome,
3916 From this day furth, for any benefice,
Bot gif it be for greit Archbischopries.
As for the rest, na money gais at all,
For the incressing of thair dignities,
3920 Na mair nor did to Peter nor to Paull.

    14. Considering *th*at our Preists, for the maist
    part,
Thay want the gift of Chastitie, we se,—
Cupido hes sa perst them throch the hart,—
3924 We grant them licence and frie libertie
That thay may haue fair Virgins to thair wyfis,
And sa keip matrimoniall Chastitie,
And nocht in huirdome for to leid thair lyfis.

3928   15. This Parliament, richt sa, hes done
    conclude,
From this day forth, our Barrouns temporall
Sall na mair mix thair nobil ancient blude
With bastard bairns of Stait Spirituall.
3932 Ilk stait amang thair awin selfis marie sall.
Gif Nobils marie with the Spritualitie,
From thyne, subiect thay salbe, and all
Sal be degraithit of thair Nobilitie,

Marginal notes:

to exact heriots.

All persons having the cure of souls are, for the good of those under them, to confine themselves to their charges, ministering as is due.

In time to come, no more money is to go to Rome, for offices in the Church, Archbishoprics excepted. SS. Peter and Paul are, herein, to be your example.

As our priests, for the most part, want the gift of chastity, they may marry maids, and so avoid sinful lives.

Barons are no longer to marry the illegitimate children of prelates.

Noblemen offending by such unions shall be disennobled,

and shall so
remain until,
on payment
of a fine, they be
rehabilitated.

In like manner,
ecclesiastics are
to find wives
in their own
order, after
ancient
precedent.

Such are the
Acts of this
Parliament.
Let them
be obeyed.
None but the
malicious will
resist them.

3936 And from amang the Nobils cancellit,
      Vnto the tyme thay by thair libertie,
      Rehabilit be the ciuill magistrate.
      And sa sall marie the Spiritualitie :
3940 Bischops with bischops sall mak affinitie ;
      Abbots and Priors, with the Priores ;
      As Bischop Annas—in Scripture we may se,—
      Maryit his dochter on Bischop Caiphas.
3944 Now haue ʒe heard the Acts honorabill
      Devysit in this present Parliament,
      To Common-weill, we think, agreabill.
      All faithfull folk sould heirof be content
3948 Them till observe with hartlie trew intent.
      I wait nane will against our Acts rebell,
      Nor till our law be inobedient,
      Bot Plutois band, the potent prince of hell.

(*Heir sall Pauper cum befoir the King, and say :*)

PAVPER.

My blessing
for your bounty
and for your
noble Acts !

May you use
them well.
Obeyed, they
will benefit;
declared, they
should be
observed.
But behead
Deceit and his
companions,
and banish
Flattery, the
scoundrel.
Then we had, all,
better rest.

3952 I gif ʒow my braid bennesoun,
      That hes givin Common-weill a goun.
      I wald nocht, for ane pair of plackis,
      ʒe had nocht maid thir nobill Actis.
3956 I pray to God and sweit Sanct Geill
      To gif ʒow grace to vse them weill.
      Wer thay weill keipit, I vnderstand,
      It war great honour to Scotland.
3960 It had bene als gude ʒe had sleipit,
      As to mak acts, and be nocht keipit.
      Bot I beseik ʒow, for Alhallows,
      To heid Dissait, and hang his fellows,
3964 And banische Flattrie aff the toun ;
      For thair was never sic ane loun.
      That beand done, I hauld it best
      That everie man ga to his rest.

CORRECTIOVN.

3968 As thou hes said, it salbe done.   It shall be so.

Suyith ! Sergeants, hang ʒon swingeours sone.   Sergeants !

(Heir sal the Sergeants lous the presoners out of the stocks, and leid them to the gallows.)

FIRST SERGEANT.

Cum heir, sir Theif ; cum heir, cum heir.   Here, Thief !

Quhen war ʒe wont to be sa sweir ?   You were not so slow in

3972 To hunt Cattell ʒe war, ay, speidie ;   stealing.

Thairfoir ʒe sall weaue in ane widdie.   You must swing.

THIFT.

Man I be hangit ? Allace ! allace !   Will no one

Is thair nane heir may get me grace ?   save me ?

3976 ʒit or I die, gif me ane drink.   Give me a drink.

FIRST SERGEANT.

Fy ! huirsun carle. I feil ane stink.   Phew !

THIFT.

Thocht I wald nocht that it war wittin,   You can tell

Sir, in gude faith I am bedirtin.   what has happened,

3980 To wit the veritie, gif ʒe pleis,   if you use

Louse doun my hois, put in ʒour neis.   your nose.

FIRST SERGEANT.

Thou art an limmer, I stand foird.   Rascal, slip your head into

Slip in thy head into this coird ;   this cord,—a

3984 For thou had never ane meiter tippit.   good fit.

THIFT.

Allace ! This is ane fellon rippit.   A bad go, this !

(Pausa.)

The widdifow wairdanis tuke my geir,   I have been

And left me nether hors nor meir,   stripped of

all ; and now I must be hanged.	3988	Nor earthlie gude that me belangit.
		Now, walloway ! I man be hangit.
Repent,		Repent ʒour lyfis, ʒe plaine oppressours,
evil-doers ;		All ʒe misdoars, and transgressours ;
or else confess,	3992	Or ellis gar chuse ʒow gude confessours,
and make ready.		And mak ʒow forde :
If you stay, and if Correction lays hands on you,		For, gif ʒe tarie in this land, And cum vnder Correctiouns hand,
a noose will be	3996	ʒour grace salbe, I vnderstand,
your grace.		Ane gude scharp coird.
Farewell,		Adew ! my bretheren, common theifis,
fellow-thieves !		That helpit me in my mischeifis.
Farewell,	4000	Adew ! Grosars, Nicksons, and Bellis :
ye cunning		Oft haue we run outthoart the fellis.
in our craft,		Adew ! Robsonis, Hansles, and Pyllis,
nimble of		That in our craft hes mony wylis,
foot, strong	4004	Lytils, Trumbels, and Armestrangs.
of hand, whose		Adew ! all theifis that me belangs,
names are so		Tailʒeours, Curwings, and Elwands,
many that I		Speidie of fut, and wicht of hands,—
have no time	4008	The Scottis of Ewisdaill, and the Graimis :
to repeat them !		I haue na tyme to tell ʒour namis.
If Correction catches you, it will be all up with you.		With King Correctioun and ʒe be fangit, Beleif, richt weill, ʒe wilbe hangit.

FIRST SERGEANT.

Make haste !	4012	Speid hand, man, with thy clitter clatter.

THIFT.

But give me		For Gods saik, sir, let me mak watter.
time to		Howbeit I haue bene cattel-gredie,
relieve nature.		It schamis to pische into ane widdie.

(Heir sal Thift be drawin vp, or his figour.)

SECVND SERGEANT.

Deceit !	4016	Cum heir, Dissait, my companʒeoun.

156

Saw ever ane man lyker ane loun,
To hing vpon ane gallows?

What a rascal
to hang!

DISSAIT.

This is aneuch to make me mangit.
4020 Duill fell me, that I man be hangit!
Let me speik with my fallows.
I trow wan-fortune brocht me heir.
Quhat mekill feind maid me sa speidie?
4024 Sen it was said, it is sevin ʒeir,
That I sould weaue into ane widdie.
I leirit my maisters to be gredie.
Adew! for I se na remeid.
4028 Luke quhat it is to be evil-deidie.

I am stunned.
I to be hanged?
Let me speak.
I am unlucky.
Seven years
ago it was
foretold I should
be hanged.
I taught greed.
I am done for.
This comes of
evil courses.

SECVND SERGEANT.

Now in this halter slip thy heid.
Stand still. Me think ʒe draw aback.

Slip your head in.
Do you flinch?

DISSAIT.

Allace! Maister, ʒe hurt my crag,

You hurt
my neck.

SECVND SERGEANT.

4032 It will hurt better, I woid an plak,
Richt now, quhen ʒe hing on ane knag.

It will hurt
more directly.

DISSAIT.

Adew! my maisters, merchant men.
I haue ʒow servit, as ʒe ken,
4036   Truelie, baith air and lait.
I say to ʒow, for conclusioun,
I dreid ʒe gang to confusioun,
Fra tyme ʒe want Dissait.
4040 I leirit ʒow, merchants, mony ane wyle,
Vpalands wyfis for to begyle,
Vpon ane markit-day,

Farewell,
merchantmen,
whom I have
served well!
You will fare
ill, without
Deceit.
I taught you
to cheat the
country wives,

and to palm off on them worthless wares for sound.	And gar them trow зour stuffe ·was gude, **4044** Quhen it was rottin,—be the Rude !— And sweir it was nocht sway.
I was always whispering you, and putting you up to tricks.	I was ay roundand in зour ear, And leirit зow for to ban and sweir **4048** Quhat зour geir cost in France, Howbeit the Devill ane word was trew.
It is well that Correction knows not of your craft.	зour craft gif King Correctioun knew, Wald turne зow to mischance.
I taught you to mix new wine and old;	**4052** I leirit зow wyllis many fauld : · To mix the new wyne and the auld,—
to buy cheap and sell dear;	That faschioun was na follie ;— To sell richt deir, and by gude chaip ;
and the art of adulteration.	**4056** And mix Ry-meill amang the saip, And Saiffrone with Oyl-dolie.
Remember usury, imitating your betters.	Forзet nocht ocker, I counsall зow, Mair then the vicker dois the kow, **4060** Or Lords thair doubill maill.
Never mind scant measure or short weight.	Howbeit зour elwand be too skant, Or зour pound-wecht thrie vnces want, Think that bot lytill faill.
Good-bye, old friends. I was true to you; and you will grieve for me, especially Tom Williamson.	**4064** Adew ! the greit Clan Iamesone, The blude Royal of Clappertoun : I was, ay, to зow trew. Baith Andersone and Paterson **4068** Above them all, Thome Williamsone, My absence зe will rew.
Tom, pray for me heartily, and reflect on my doings ; for you learned from me how to cheat the Bishop and his clerks.	Thome Williamsone, it is зour pairt To pray for me with all зour hairt, **4072** And think vpon my warks ; How I leirit зow ane gude lessoun, For to begyle, in Edinburgh toun, The Bischop and his Clarks.
Young merchants, you may curse yonder king.	**4076** зe, зoung merchants, may cry allace : For wanting of зour wonted grace, зon curst King зe may ban.

Had I leifit bot halfe ane ȝeir,
4080 I sould haue leirit ȝow crafts perqueir,
To begyle wyfe and man.

In six months more I would have made you adepts.

How may ȝe, merchants, mak debait,
Fra tyme ȝe want ȝour man Dissait ?
4084 For ȝow I mak great cair.

You will strive fruitlessly, without Deceit.

Without I ryse fra deid to lyfe,
I wait weill, ȝe will never thryfe
Farther nor the fourth air.

Unless I come to life, you will not thrive many generations.

(Heir sal Dissait be drawin vp, or ellis his figure.)

FIRST SERGEANT.

4088 Cum heir, Falset, & mense the gallows.
ȝe man hing vp amang ȝour fallows,
For ȝour cankart conditioun.

Come, Falsehood, and grace the gallows, with your mates.

Monie ane trew man haue ȝe wrangit :
4092 Thairfoir, but doubt, ȝe salbe hangit,
But mercie or remissioun.

For your wrongdoing you must swing.

FALSET.

Allace ! Man I be hangit, to ?
Quhat mekill Devil is this ado ?
4096 How came I to this cummer ?

How did I incur this nuisance of being hanged ?

My gude maisters, ȝe craftsmen,
Want ȝe Falset, full weill I ken,
ȝe will, all, die for hunger.

Craftsmen, you will starve, without Falsehood.

4100 ȝe, men of craft, may cry allace.
Quhen ȝe want me, ȝe want ȝour grace ;
Thairfoir, put into wryte
My lessouns that I did ȝow leir.

As you will miss me, note down my instructions.

4104 Howbeit the commons eyne ȝe bleir,
Count ȝe nocht that ane myte.

Don't mind practising guile.

Find me ane Wobster that is leill,
Or ane Walker that will nocht steill,—
4108 Thair craftines I ken,—

Is any weaver or fuller honest ?

A miller that

will not steal you

may count holy.

Among butchers,

to blow up their

meat is only

a joke:

and I taught

it to them.

Tailors, too,

learned from me,

in the towns.

Country tailors

I allowed

to cabbage.

Andro Fortoun

will be frantic

about me;

and Tailor

Babarage will

roar at seeing

me hanged.

Not so Deacon

Jamie Ralfe,

honest fool;

nor Willie

Cadyeoch, the

selfish maltworm.

To the brewers

of Cowpertown

I leave a

hearty curse.

They think it

no harm to brew

washy ale.

Do you know

how they make

harns-out?

Or ane Millair that hes na falt,
That will nather steill meall nor malt,
    Hauld them for halie men.
4112 At our fleschers tak ʒe na greife.
Thocht thay blaw leane mutton and beife,
    That thay seime fat and fair,
Thay think that practick bot ane mow.
4116 Howbeit the Devill a thing it dow,
    To thame I leirit that lair.
I leirit Tailʒeours, in everie toun,
To schaip fyue quarters in ane goun,
4120   In Angus, and in Fyfe.
To vplands Tailʒeours I gaue gude leife
To steill ane sillie stump, or sleife,
    Vnto Kittok, his wyfe.
4124 My gude maister, Audro Fortoun,
Of Tailʒeours that may weir the croun,
    For me he will be mangit.
Tailʒeour Babarage, my sone and air,
4128 I wait, for me will rudlie rair,
    Fra tyme he se me hangit.
The barfit Deacon, Iamie Ralfe,
Quha never ʒit bocht kow nor calfe,
4132   Becaus he can nocht steall;
Willie Cadʒeoch will make na plead,
Howbeit his wyfe want beife and bread,
    Get he gude barmie aill.
4136 To the brousters of Cowper toun
I leife my braid black malesoun,
    Als hartlie as I may.
To make thinne aill thay think na falt,
4140 Of mekill burne and lytill malt,
    Agane the market-day.
And thay can mak, withoutin doubt,
Ane kynde of aill thay call Harns-out.
4144   Wait ʒe how thay mak that?

160

Ane curtill queine, ane laidlie lurdane,
Of strang wesche scho will tak ane iurdane,
And settis in the gyle-fat.

4148 Quha drinks of that aill, man or page,
It will gar all his harnis rage.

That iurdane I may rew :
It gart my heid rin hiddie giddie.

4152 Sirs, God ! nor I die in ane widdie,
Gif this taill be nocht trew.

Speir at the Sowtar, Geordie Sillie,
Fra tyme that he had fild his bellie
4156 With this vnhelthsum aill.

Than all the Baxters will I ban,
That mixes bread with dust and bran,
And fyne flour with beir maill.

4160 Adew ! my maisters, Wrichts and Maissouns.
I haue neid to leir ʒow few lessouns :
ʒe knaw my craft perqueir.

Adew ! blak-Smythis and Loriners.

4164 Adew ! ʒe craftie Cordiners,
That sellis the schone over deir.

Gold Smythis, fair-weill ! aboue them all.
Remember my memoriall,
4168 With mony ane sittill cast.

To mix, set ʒe nocht by twa preinis,
Fyne Ducat gold with hard Gudlingis,
Lyke as I leirnit ʒow last.

4172 Quhen I was ludgit vpaland,
The Schiphirds maid with me ane band,
Richt craftelie to steill.

Than did I gif ane confirmatioun
4176 To all the Schiphirdis of this Natioun,
That thay sould never be leill,
And ilk ane to reset ane vther.

I knaw fals Schiphirds, fyftie fidder,—
4180 War thair canteleinis kend,—

How thay mak, in thair conventiouns,

On montans, far fra ony touns,

To let them never mend.

4184 Amang craftsmen, it is ane wonder

To find ten leill amang ane hunder :

The treuth I to 3ow tell.

Adew ! I may na langer tarie.

4188 I man pas to the King of Farie,

Or ellis the rycht to hell.

(*Heir sall he luke vp to his fallows hingand.*)

Wa is me ! For the gude common thift,

Was never man maid ane mair honest schift

4192 His leifing for to win.

Thair was nocht ane, in all Lidsdaill,

That ky mair craftelie culd staill,

Quhair thou hings on that pin.

4196 Sathan ressaue thy saull, Dissait !

Thou was to me ane faithfull mait,

And, als, my father brother.

Duill fell the sillie merchant men!

4200 To mak them service, weill I ken,

Thaill never get sic ane vther.

(*Heir sall thay festin the coard to his neck, with ane dum
countenance. Thairefter, he sall say :*)

Gif any man list for to be my mait,

Cum follow me ; for I am at the gait.

4204 Cum follow me, all catyfe, covetous Kings,

Reauers, but richt, of vthers Realmis and Rings,

Togidder with all wrangous conquerours.

And bring, with 3ow all publick oppressours,

4208 With Pharao, King of Egiptians :

With him, in hell, salbe 3our recompence.

All cruell schedders of blude innocent,

Cum follow me ; or ellis rin and repent.

4212 Prelats that hes ma benefeits nor thrie,

And will nocht teich nor preiche the veritie, and idle prelates,

Without at God, in tyme, thay cry for grace, unrepenting,

In hiddeous hell I sall prepair thair place. will be lost.

4216 Cum follow me, all fals corruptit Iudges. Come, false judges,

With Pontius Pilat I sall prepair 3our ludges. and Pontius Pilate.

All 3e officials that parts men with thair wyfis, Ye that part

Cum follow me ; or els gang mend 3our lyfis ;— man and wife,

4220 With all fals leiders of the constrie law, that abuse

With wanton Scribs and Clarks, intill ane raw, the law to

That to the puir maks mony partiall traine, the injury

Syne, hodie ad octo bids them cum againe. of the poor,

4224 And 3e that taks rewairds at baith the hands, and that take bribes, must go

3e sall, with me, be bund in Baliels bands. with me.

Cum follow me, all curst vnhappie wyfis, Unfaithful wives,

That with 3our gudemen dayly flytis and stryfis, who vex their

4228 And quyetlie with rybalds makes repair, husbands and wrong them,

And taks na cure to make ane wrangous air. will be rewarded

3e sal, in hel, rewairdit be, I wein, in hell, with

With Iesabell, of Israell the Queene. Jezebel.

4232 I haue ane curst vnhappie wyfe, my sell. And what a

Wald God scho war befoir me into hell ! wife I have!

That Bismair, war scho thair, withoutin doubt, She would turn the Devil himself

Out of hell the Devill scho wald ding out. out of hell.

4236 3e maryit men, evin as 3e luife 3our lyfis, Married men,

Let never preists be hamelie with 3our wyfis. beware of priests.

My wyfe with preists sho doith me greit onricht, Me they have cuckolded

And maid me nine tymes cuckald, on ane nicht. roundly.

4240 Fairweil ! For I am to the widdie wend ; Good-bye! Falsehood never made a

For quhy falset maid never ane better end. better end.

(Heir sal he be heisit vp, and not his figure ; and an Craw or ane Ke salbe castin vp, as it war his saull.)

FLATTRIE.

Haue I nocht chaipit the widdie weil ? How well I have escaped

3ea, that I haue, be sweit Sanct Geill ! scragging !

163

For I deserved **4244**

For I had nocht bene wrangit ;

it even more

Becaus I servit,—be Alhallows !—

richly than my

Till haue bene merchellit amang my fellowis,

companions,

And heich aboue them hangit.

in that I **4248**

I maid far ma falts nor my maits :

beguiled the

I begylde all the thrie estaits

three Estates.

With my hypocrisie.

With my hood
on, I was
thought good. **4252**

Quhen I had on my freirs hude,

All men beleifit that I was gude.

Am I !

Now iudge ȝe gif I be.

Let the greatest

Tak me an rackles rubyatour,

of rascals

Ane theif, ane tyrane, or ane tratour,

only don a **4256**
friar's dress,

Of everie vyce the plant ;

and the wives

Gif him the habite of ane freir,

will deem him

The wyfis will trow, withoutin weir,

a very saint.

He be ane verie Saint.

That dress **4260**

I knaw that cowle and skaplarie

covers more

Genners mair hait nor charitie,

heat than charity.

Thocht thay be blak or blew.

Is a wolf

Quhat halines is thair within

in a sheep's **4264**

Ane wolfe cled in ane wedders skin ?

skin holy ?

Iudge ȝe gif this be trew.

But, escaped,

Sen I haue chaipit this firie farie,

I will not stay

Adew ! I will na langer tarie,

to chatter. **4268**

To cumber ȝow with my clatter ;

I will go,
humbly, and
teach the Hermit
of Loretto how
to flatter.

Bot I will, with ane humbill spreit,

Gang serve the Hermeit of Lareit,

And leir him for till flatter.

(Heir sal enter Foly.)

FOLIE.

Good-day ! Don't **4272**
you return
any salute ?
Drunk fools
are glad.
Don't you
know me ?

Gude day, my Lords, and, als, God saine !

Dois na man bid gude day againe ?

Quhen fuillis ar fow, then ar thay faine,

Ken ȝe nocht me ?

4276 How call thay me can ȝe nocht tell ?
  Now, be him that herryit hell !
  I wait nocht how thay call my sell,
    Bot gif I lie.

My name ?
I don't know,
myself, unless
I lie.

DILIGENCE.

4280 Quhat brybour is this that maks sic beiris ?

What beggarly
wretch is this ?

FOLIE.

  The feind ressaue that mouth that speirs !
  Gude-man, ga play ȝow with ȝour feiris,
    With muck vpon ȝour mow.

Out on you that !
ask ! Go and
play with
your fellows.

DILIGENCE.

4284 Fond fuill, quhair hes thou bene sa lait ?

Where have
you been so late ?

FOLIE.

  Marie ! Cummand throw the Schogait.
  Bot thair hes bene ane great debait
    Betwixt me and ane Sow.

I have had
a quarrel
with a sow.

4288 The Sow cryit guff, and I, to-ga :
  Throw speid of fute, I gat awa ;
  Bot, in the midst of the cawsa,
    I fell into ane midding.

I managed to
run away, but
fell into a
dung-heap.

4292 Scho lap vpon me, with ane bend.
  Quhaever the middings sould amend,
  God send them ane mischevous end !
    For that is bot Gods bidding ;

She sprang
on me.
Bless the
dung-heaps !

4296 As I was pudlit thair, God wait,
  Bot with my club I maid debait,
  Ise never cum againe that gait,
    I sweir ȝow, be Alhallows !

Bemired there,
if I had not
had my club,
I should never
have saved
myself.

4300 I wald the officiars of the toun,
  That suffers sic confusioun,
  That thay war harbreit with Mahown,
    Or hangit on ane gallows.

The officers of
the town should
be made to rue
it for their
negligence.

      ll

The Devil take those who leave the country uncared-for!

4304   Fy, fy, that sic ane fair cuntrie
Sould stand sa lang but policie !
I gif them to the Devill, hartlie,
     That hes the wyte.

I wish the Provost would look to the dung-heap where I met my mischance.

4308   I wald the Provost wald tak in heid
Of ȝon midding to make remeid,
Quhilk pat me and the Sow at feid.
     Quhat may I do bot flyte ?

REX HVMANITAS.

Diligence, bring yonder fool hither.

4312   Pas on, my servant Diligence,
And bring ȝon fuill to our presence.

DILIGENCE.

At once.

Folly, go to the King.

That sall be done, but tarying.
Foly, ȝe man ga to the King.

FOLIE.

Is that he, with the gilt cap ?

4316   The King ? Quhat kynde of thing is that ?
Is ȝon he, with the goldin Hat ?

DILIGENCE.

Yes. Come along.

ȝon same is he.   Cum on thy way.

FOLIE.

Good-day !

I have a complaint to make.

Gif ȝe be King, God ȝow gude day.
4320   I haue ane plaint to make to ȝow.

REX HVMANITAS.

Against whom ?

Quhom on, Folie ?

FOLIE.

A sow.

She has sworn to slay or to maim me.

You should do justice to all.

Marie ! On ane Sow.
Sir, scho hes sworne that scho sall sla me,
4324   Or ellis byte baith my balloks fra me.
Gif ȝe be King,—be Sanct Allan !—
ȝe sould do Iustice to ilk man.

Had I nocht keipit me with my club,

4328 The Sow had drawin me in ane dub.

I heir them say thair is cum to the toun

Ane King, callit Correctioun.

I pray ȝow tell me quhilk is he.

My club alone
saved me.
Which is King
Correction, who,
they say, has
come to town ?

DILIGENCE.

4332 Ȝon, with the wings. May nocht se ?

He with the
wings.

FOLIE.

Now, wallie fall that weill fairde mow !

Sir, I pray ȝow correct ȝon Sow,

Quhilk with hir teith, but sword or knyfe,

4336 Had maist haue reft me of my lyfe.

Gif ȝe will nocht mak correctioun,

Than gif me ȝour protectioun

Of all Swyne for to be skaithles,

4340 Betuix this toun and Invernes.

Bless him !
Sire, correct
yonder sow
for all but
killing me.
If you will not,
then protect me
from all swine
between here
and Inverness.

DILIGENCE.

Foly, hes thou ane wyfe at hame ?

Have you a wife ?

FOLIE.

Ȝea, that I haue, God send hir schame !

I trow, be this, scho is neir deid :

4344 I left ane wyfe bindand hir heid.

To schaw hir seiknes I think schame.

Scho hes sic rumbling in hir wambe,

That all the nicht my hart overcasts

4348 With bocking and with thunder-blasts.

Yes, and nearly
dead, I imagine.
I don't know
what has come
to her; but she
was in a very
bad way all the
night long.

DILIGENCE.

Peradventure scho be with bairne.

Perhaps she
is pregnant.

FOLIE.

Allace ! I trow scho be forfairne.

Scho sobbit, and scho fell in sown ;

She is almost
worn out, I
think.

She fell into
a swoon; and
then they
rubbed her up
and down;
and then she
got some
comfort, but
to the great
discomfort of
everybody
around.
And she was
quite unable
to control
herself.

4352   And than thay rubbit hir vp and doun.
Scho riftit, routit, and maid sic stends,
Scho ȝeild, and gaid at baith the ends,
Till scho had castin ane cuppill of quarts ;
4356   Syne, all turnit to ane rickill of farts.
Scho blubert, bockit, and braikit still ;
Hir arsse gaid evin lyke ane wind-mill.
Scho stumblit, and stutterit, with sic stends,
4360   That scho recantit at baith the ends.
Sik dismell drogs fra hir scho schot,
Quhill scho maid all the fluir on flot.
Of hir hurdies scho had na hauld,
4364   Quhill scho had twmed hir mony fauld.

DILIGENCE.

You had better
take her to
the doctors.

Better bring hir to the Leitches heir.

FOLIE.

Pshaw! She is
not to be moved,
she is in such
a condition ;
and she con-
stantly cries
for a priest.

Trittill trattill ! Scho may nocht steir.
Hir verie buttoks maks sic beir,
4368   It skars baith foill and fillie.
Scho bocks sik bagage fra hir breist,
He wants na bubbils that sittis hir neist ;
And ay scho cryis, a preist ! a preist !
4372   With ilk a quhillie lillie.

DILIGENCE.

Didn't she
recover at last ?

Recoverit scho nocht, at the last ?

FOLIE.

Yes, but noisily.
I pity her, when
she sighs.

ȝea ; bot, wit ȝe weil, scho fartit fast.
Bot, quhen scho sichis, my hart is sorie.

DILIGENCE.

Does she drink
at all ?

4376   Bot drinks scho ocht ?

168

FOLIE.

꒩e,—be Sanct Marie !—
Ane quart at anis it will nocht tarie,
And leif the Devill a drap.
4380 Than sic flobbage scho layis fra hir,
About the wallis, God wait, sic wair !
Quhen it was drunkin, I gat to skair
The lickings of the cap.

DILIGENCE.

4384 Quhat is in that creill, I pray the tell.

FOLIE.

Marie ! I haue Folie-Hats to sell.

DILIGENCE.

I pray the, sell me ane or tway.

FOLIE.

Na.   Tarie quhill the market-day.
4388 I will sit doun heir,—be Sanct Clune !—
And gif my babies thair disiune.
Cum heir, gude Glaiks, my dochter deir.
Thou salbe maryit, within ane ꒩eir,
4392 Vpon ane freir of Tillilum.
Na : thou art nather deaf nor dum.
Cum hidder, Stult, my sone and air.
My ioy, thou art baith gude and fair.
4396 Now sall I fend ꒩ow as I may,
Thocht ꒩e cry lyke ane Ke all day.

(*Heir sal the bairns cry keck, lyke ane Kae ; and he sal put meat
in thair mouth.*)

DILIGENCE.

Get vp, Folie, but tarying,
And speid ꒩ow, haistelie, to the King.
4400 Get vp.   Me think the carle is dum.

FOLIE.

Bah! Bah!

Now, bum, balerie, bum, bum.

DILIGENCE.

Out of this
trance, and
get up; or
else I will take
your wallet.

Shame on you.

4404

I trow the trucour lyis in ane trance.
Get vp, man, with ane mirrie mischance;
Or—be Sanct Dyonis of France !—
    Ise gar the want thy wallet.
It's schame to se, man, how thow lyis.

FOLIE.

If I get up
again I will
break your pate.

I am overcome
at sight of
yonder fair lass
in a satin gown.

If I had you in
a quiet place,
you would not
wish to run away.

You pretty-armed
thing, I should
like to kiss
your lips.

Angry as you
look, if chance
favoured, you
would try
my mettle.

4408

4412

4416

4420

4424

Wa ! 3it againe ? Now, this is thryis.
The Devill wirrie me, and I ryse,
    Bot I sall break thy pallet.
Me think my pillok will nocht ly doun.
Hauld doun 3our head, 3e lurdon loun.
3on fair las with the Sating goun
    Gars 3ow thus bek and bend.
Take, thair, ane neidill for 3our cace.
Now, for all the hiding of 3our face,
Had I 3ow in ane quyet place,
    3e wald nocht waine to flend.
Thir bony armis, that ar cled in silk,
Ar evin als wantoun as any wilk.
I wald forbeir baith bread and milk,
    To kis thy bony lippis.
Suppois 3e luke as 3e war wraith,
War 3e at quyet behind ane claith,
3e wald not stick to preife my graith
    With hobling of 3our hippis.

DILIGENCE.

Come to the
King, and stop
your prating.

Here is Folly, the
lazy scamp.

4428

Suyith ! harlot. Haist the to the King,
And let allane thy trattilling.
Lo ! heir is Folie, sir, alreadie,—
Ane richt sweir swingeour, be our Ladie !

FOLIE.

Thou art not half sa sweir, thy sell.

Quhat meins this pulpit, I pray the tell.

And you?
What means this pulpit?

DILIGENCE.

4432 Our new Bischops hes maid ane preiching;

Bot thou heard never sic pleasant teiching.

ʒon Bischop wil preich throch the coast.

Our new Bishops preach. You never heard such pleasant instruction.

FOLIE.

Than stryk ane hag into the poast;

4436 For I hard never, in all my lyfe,

Ane Bischop cum to preich in Fyfe.

Gif Bischops to be preichours leiris,

Wallaway! quhat sall word of freiris?

4440 Gif Prelats preich in brugh and land,

The sillie freirs, I vnderstand.

Thay will get na mair meall nor malt;

Sa, I dreid, freirs sall die for falt.

4444 Sen sa is, that ʒon nobill King

Will mak men Bischops for preiching,

Quhat say ʒe, sirs? Hauld ʒe nocht best

That I gang preich, amang the rest?

4448 Quhen I haue preichit on my best wayis,

Then will I sell my merchandise

To my bretherin and tender maits

That dwels amang the thrie estaits;

4452 For I haue, heir, gude chaifery

Till any fuill that lists to by.

Note that; for I never heard of the like. If Bishops learn to preach, I suspect that the friars will starve to death. If that King gives bishoprics for preaching, why should not I preach? After preaching as best I can, I will go sell my wares among the three Estates, to any fool that will buy.

(*Heir sall Foly hing vp his hattis on the pulpet, and say :*)

God sen I had ane Doctours hude!

I wish I had a doctor's hood.

REX HVMANITAS.

Quhy, Folie? Wald thou mak ane preiching?

Would you preach?

FOLIE.

I would, and in plain words.

4456 3ea, that I wald, sir,—be the Rude!—
But eyther flattering or fleiching.

REX HVMANITAS.

Let us hear what he says.

Now, brother, let vs heir his teiching,—
To pas our tyme,—and heir him raife.

DILIGENCE.

The kitchen and the pots best befit him.

Shall I act as

clerk for you?

4460 He war far meiter for the kitching,
Amang the pottis, sa Christ me saife!
Fond Foly, sall I be thy Clark,
And answeir the, ay, with amen?

FOLIE.

First, the fiend take that . ugly face!

4464 Now, at the beginning of my wark,
The feind ressaue that graceles grim!

(Heir sal Folie begin his sermon, as followis :)

Solomon, the

wisest King

of Israel, has

said that fools

are innumerable;

and I am not

ashamed to be

one, since there

are so many.

     Stultorum numerus infinitus.
Salomon, the maist sapient King,
4468 In Israell quhan he did ring,
Thir words, in effect, did write :
The number of fuillis ar infinite.
I think na schame—sa Christ me saife !—
4472 To be ane fuill, amang the laife,
Howbeit ane hundreth stands heir by,
Perventure als great fuillis as I.
     Stultorum.

I have kindred

in every land,

Earls, Dukes,

Kings, &c.,—

fools now, as

they have

long been.

4476 I haue, of my Genelogie,
Dwelland in everie cuntrie,
Earles, Duiks, Kings, and Empriours,
With mony guckit Conquerours,
4480 Quhilk dois in Folie perseveir,
And hes done sa this many 3eir.

Sum seiks to warldlie dignities,
And sum, to sensuall vanities.

4484 Quhat vails all thir vaine honours,
Nocht being sure to leife twa houris ?

Sum greidie fuill dois fill ane box ;
Ane vther fuill cummis, and breaks the lox,

4488 And spends that vther fuillis hes spaird,
Quhilk never thocht on them to wairde.

Sum dois as thay sould never die.
Is nocht this folie ? Quhat say ȝe ?

4492 Sapientia huius mundi stultitia est apud
Deum.

Becaus thair is sa many fuillis
Rydand on hors, and, sum, on muillis,

Heir I haue bocht gude chafery

4496 Till ony fuill that lists to by,
And, speciallie, for the thrie estaits,
Quhair I haue mony tender maits ;
Quhilk causit them, as ȝe may se,

4500 Gang backwart throw the haill cuntrie.
Gif with my merchandise ȝe list to mell,
Heir I haue Folie-Hattis to sell.
Quhairfoir is this Hat, wald ȝe ken ?

4504 Marie ! For insatiabill merchant men.
Quhen God hes send them abundance,
Ar nocht content with sufficiance,
Bot saillis into the stormy blastis,

4508 In Winter to get greater castis,—
In mony terribill great torment,
Against the Acts of Parliament.
Sum tynis thair geir, and sum ar drounde :

4512 With this sic merchants sould be crounde.

DILIGENCE.

Quhom to schaips thou to sell that hude ?
I trow, to sum great man of gude.

They aim after
unsubstantial
things, though
life is quite
uncertain.

One fool hoards
gold; and
another fool
steals and
spends it.

Others are so
foolish as to
act as if they
were never to die.

There being
many wealthy
fools,

I have bought

goods for them,

and, especially,
for the three
Estates, in which
I have many
mates, as appears
from their acts.

I have fools-
caps to sell.

This one is for

the merchants.

Not content with
abundance,
they run risks
in winter-time,
in the teeth
of the Acts of
Parliament,
with various
results.

This cap
suits such.

And this hood
is for some
rich man ?

FOLIE.

I would sell it	This hude to sell richt faine I wald
to some one	4516 Till him that is baith auld & cald,
old and cold,	Reddie till pas to hell, or heavin,
ready to die,	
with a family	And hes fair bairns, sax or seavin,
of children,	And is of age fourscoir of ʒeir,
and who, yet,	4520 And taks ane lasse to be his peir,
weds a mere	Quhilk is nocht fourteine ʒeir of age,
girl, trusting	
that she will	And ioynis with hir in mariage,
not make him	Geifand hir traist that scho nocht wald
a cuckold.	4524 Rycht haistelie mak him cuckald.
For the like	Quha maryes, beand sa neir thair dead,
of him this	
cap is suited.	Set on this Hat vpon his head.

DILIGENCE.

What cap is this?   Quhat Hude is that, tell me I pray the.

FOLIE.

This cap is holy	4528 This is ane haly Hude, I say the.
and ordained,	This Hude is ordanit, I the assure,
and is for	For Sprituall fuillis that taks in cure
spiritual fools	The saullis of great Diosies,
who, unfit, under-	
take cures from	4532 And regiment of great Abesies,
mere motives	For gredines of warldlie pelfe,
of gain,	Than can nocht iustlie gyde them selfe.
and sell them-	Vthers sauls to saife it settis them weill,
selves to Satan.	4536 Syne, sell thair awin saullis to the Deuill.
This cap is	Quhaever dois sa, this I conclude,
proper for such.	Vpon his heid set on this Hude.

DILIGENCE.

Are such in the	Foly, is thair ony sic men
Church now ?	
How shall I	4540 Now in the Kirk, that thou can ken ?
recognize them ?	How sall I ken them ?

FOLIE.

Na, keip that clois.

Ex operibus eorum cognoscetis eos.

4544 And fuillis speik of the Prelacie,
It will be hauldin for herisie.

Know them by their works.

It is heresy to speak of the prelates.

REX HVMANITAS.

Speik on hardlie. I gif the leife.

I give you leave to speak.

FOLIE.

Than my remissioun is in my sleife.

4548 Will 3e leife me to speik of Kings?

Then I am safe.

May I speak of kings?

REX HVMANITAS.

3ea : hardlie speik of all kin things.

Yes, of all the like.

[FOLIE.]

Conforming to my first narratioun,
3e ar, all, fuillis, be Coks passioun!

As I said before, you are, all, fools.

DILIGENCE.

4552 Thou leis. I trow this fuill be mangit.

A lie. He is demented.

FOLIE.

Gif I lie, God! nor thou be hangit.
For I haue heir—I to the tell,—
Ane nobill cap imperiell,

4556 Quhilk is nocht ordanit bot for doings
Of Empreours, of Duiks, and Kings,—
For princelie and imperiall fuillis :
Thay sould haue luggis als lang as Muillis.

4560 The pryde of Princes, withoutin faill,
Gars all the warld rin top ovir taill.
To win them warldlie gloir and gude,
Thay cure nocht schedding of saikles blude.

Not so.

For I have, here, a noble cap,

suited for royal fools of every

sort and description.

Princes confuse the world by their pride, and, to satisfy it, slay the innocent.

England would have troubled us sorely, but for the aid of France.

4564 Quhat cummer haue ȝe had, in Scotland,
Be our auld enemies of Ingland ?
Had nocht bene the support of France,
We had bene brocht to great mischance.

And now the Emperor is going to blows with France.

4568 Now, I heir tell, the Empreour,
Schaippis for till be ane Conquerour,
And is muifing his ordinance
Against the Nobill King of France.

His reason I know not

4572 Bot I knaw nocht his iust querrell,
That he hes for till mak battell.

Princes in general are, this year, in a commotion, which some will regret.

All the Princes of Almanie,
Spainȝe, Flanders, and Italie,
4576 This present ȝeir, ar in ane flocht :
Sum sall thair wages find deir bocht.

The Pope has sent his army into the field, outdoing the old Saints.

The Paip, with bombard, speir, and scheild,
Hes send his armie to the feild.
4580 Sanct Peter, Sanct Paull, nor Sanct Androw
Raisit never sic ane Oist, I trow.

Is this charity ?

Is this fraternall charitie ?

Or is it folly ?

Or furious folie ? Quhat say ȝe ?

Christ taught not this foolishness; for such it is, among Christians.

4584 Thay leird nocht this at Christis Scuillis :
Thairfoir, I think them verie fuillis.
I think it folie,—be Gods mother !—
Ilk Christian Prince to ding doun vther.

For them is this cap.

4588 Becaus that this hat sould belang them,
Gang thou, and part it evin amang them.

Fulfilled, now, is Merlin's prophecy,

The Prophesie, withouttin weir,
Of Merling beis compleit this ȝeir.

which I learnt from my grandmother ;

4592 For my gudame, the Gyre Carling,
Leirnde me the Prophesie of Marling ;

and thus it runs.

Quhairof I sall schaw the sentence,
Gif ȝe will gif me audience :

Merlin's prophecy.

4596   Flan, Fran resurgent, simul Hispan viribus
          vrgent,
     Dani vastabunt, Vallones valla parabunt.

176

Sic tibi nomen in a mulier cacavit in olla.
Hoc epulum comedes.

DILIGENCE.

5600 Marie! That is ane il-sauorit dische.

A foul mess.

FOLIE.

Sa, be this Prophesie plainlie appeirs,   *So, friars are*

That mortall weirs salbe amang freirs.   *to wrangle;*

Thay sall nocht knaw weill, in thair closters,   *their religion*

5604 To quhom thay sall say thair Pater nosters.   *being disordered.*

Wald thay fall to, and fecht with speir and   *Would that*
    sheild,   *they fought*

The feind mak cuir quhilk of them win the   *with spear*
    feild.   *and shield!*

Now of my sermon haue I maid ane end;   *Finally I com-*

5608 To Gilly-mouband I ȝow all commend: *mend you to Gilly-moubund.*

And I ȝow all beseik, richt hartfullie,   *Pray, too, for*

Pray for the saull of gude Cacaphatie,—   *the soul of*

Quhilk laitlie drounit himself into Lochleavin,—   *Cacaphatie, who*

5612 That his sweit saull may be aboue the heavin.   *was drowned.*

DILIGENCE.

Famous peopil, hartlie I ȝow requyre   *Take our play*

This lytill sport to tak in patience.   *in good part.*

We traist to God, and we leif ane vther ȝeir,   *Next year, if we*

5616 Quhair we haue failit, we sall do diligence,   *live, we will try to do*

With mair pleasure, to mak ȝow recompence;   *better;*

Because we haue bene, sum part, tedious,   *for we have been tedious,*

With mater rude, denude of eloquence,   *rude, and, perchance,*

5620 Likewyse, perchance, to sum men odious.   *invidious.*

Now let ilk man his way avance;   *Now go, and*

Let sum ga drink, and sum ga dance: *drink, and try*

Menstrell, blaw vp ane brawll of France;   *who can dance*

5624   Let se quha hobbils best.   *best.*

For I will rin, incontinent,
To the Tavern, or ever I stent,
And pray to God omnipotent,
5628   To send ȝow all gude rest.

I, myself, will run straight to the tavern, and will pray that you may, all, have good rest.

Rex sapiens, æterne Deus, genitorque benigne,
Sit tibi, perpetuo, gloria, laus, & honor.

Glory, praise, and honour be to God evermore!

Printed at Edinburgh, be Robert Charteris.

An. Do. MDCII.

And are to be sauld in his Buith, on the North side of the Gait, at the West side of the auld Prouosts Closhead.